I0814457

‘I have greatly enjoyed these unusual and spiritually perceptive devotions for Christian academics. These short chapters are deeply rooted in the careful reading of Scripture and earthed in the author’s commitment to encouraging faithfulness in believers engaged in academic studies. Having heard many of these in our Tuesday chapels at Tyndale House, I have greatly enjoyed being reminded of the author’s pastoral concern and insightful comments, often accompanied by a lovely dry sense of humour.’
The Revd Christopher Ash, Writer in Residence, Tyndale House, Cambridge, UK

‘This book is a must read for all Christian academics, particularly for those of us who believe that Christian scholarship is fundamentally a divine calling. The messages given by Dirk at the chapel services and that are published here had a profound influence on my convictions and attitudes as an aspiring Christian academic completing my PhD studies at Tyndale House, Cambridge. They are a model of Christian scholarship that I strive to emulate in my own academic work, teaching and training in Brazil. I am unaware of anyone more careful and incisive in the application of Scripture to the realities of academic life than Dirk Jongkind.’
Dr Diego dy Carlos, Research Lecturer, Seminário Martin Bucer, Brazil

‘Has the Bible a vital message for academics? Dirk Jongkind’s devotions show that God’s word pierces with a cutting edge through the thicket of scholarship. Passages from the Old and New Testament give advice on how to keep up joy in

the often stressful environment of the university, how to deal with ambivalent motivations such as ambition, how to build an academic career on the sound ground of God's calling and character. A *must read* for everyone who pursues an academic career not only as a job, but as a vocation!'
Dr Alexander Fink, Director, Institut für Glaube und Wissenschaft, Marburg, Germany

'If you are a Christian academic and want to grow in your faith, then this little book is for you. Dirk Jongkind leads the reader carefully though nineteen passages selected from the Bible, with a detailed devotional commentary and several probing questions. Any academic that works through these passages thoughtfully and prayerfully with Dirk as guide is surely certain to find their faith increased.'
Dr Daniel J. Hill, Senior Lecturer in Philosophy, University of Liverpool, UK

'Young Christian academics often express a desire to be mentored by older scholars, but pastorally minded academics are not always available to take on that role. This book helps to fill the gap. Dirk Jongkind's decades of studying Scripture and working alongside other academics in a research institute have allowed him to become very familiar with the particular struggles academics face, and the comfort and challenge Scripture offers them. In *Growing in Understanding*, he shares what he has learned with others – and the result is a book full of fresh insights from Scripture specifically applied to the academic life. I highly recommend it, not only for academics looking for devotional material but also for postgraduate and academic fellowship groups,

since the discussion questions provided at the end of each chapter make it ideal for group study.'
Anja Lijcklama a Nijeholt, Fellows Programme Coordinator, Forming a Christian Mind, Cambridge, and Postgraduate Ministry Coordinator, UCCF and IFES Europe

'Dirk Jongkind's book *Growing in Understanding: Devotions for Christian Academics* is distilled wisdom from a gifted Cambridge University faculty member. I remember the first time I heard Dirk teach these devotionals to a group of talented young academics at the Cambridge Scholars Network. As embodied and taught by Dirk, God's word made a stunning impact on the eager, young scholars. Further, the biblical vision in this book – of how to be a Christian academic – has, over the last two decades, shaped the European Leadership Forum's vision of equipping and mentoring Christian academics for faithful and excellent work. If you read these short chapters and meditate on them and on the passages of Scripture they unpack, God can change your life, including your understanding and practice of your academic calling.'
Dr Greg Pritchard, Director, European Leadership Forum, and President, Forum of Christian Leaders, Naperville, Illinois, USA

'Postgraduate studies can often be a very isolating and lonely journey that can bring up all sorts of negative feelings and struggles, such as stress, insecurities, disillusionment and despair. Amid this internal turmoil, we can easily lose sight of how our Christian faith relates to our work. With years of academic research and association with Tyndale House, Dirk Jongkind has authored *Growing in Understanding: Devotions for Christian Academics* to encourage Christians in the academy to come to a better understanding of ourselves and the occupational hazards that we face, which can easily derail our devotion to God. Dirk helps us by providing solid, godly biblical wisdom that aids us in our research journey, focusing our gaze on God as we pursue our research. Through a careful exegesis of various biblical passages, Dirk encourages us to be devotional in our academic pursuits by helping us to understand who we are in Jesus and how that relationship with Jesus has supremacy over everything we do.'

The Revd Dr Vuyani Sindo, Vice Principal (Development) and Head of Biblical Studies, George Whitefield College, Cape Town, South Africa

'In this book, Dirk Jongkind provides an inspiring and practical guide for those who seek to reflect God's wisdom in every area of life, with a special focus on academics. I found it deeply challenging for my personal devotions as well as in mentoring young academics on how to develop biblical discernment. Having had the privilege of observing the way he lives out his convictions at home and work – through devotional times with his children and with his students at Tyndale – and now reading his book, I must testify that my love for the word of God has deepened. The selected scriptures from both the Old and New Testaments are highly relevant to our contemporary European academic context, a culture often hostile to the gospel. It was a timely reminder of the vital importance of allowing Scripture to shape my understanding of God's wisdom before engaging in academic research or mentoring students. This book left me informed, alarmed, rebuked and inspired to take action.'

Emanuel Tundrea, Associate Professor of IT, Emanuel University of Oradea, Romania

Dirk Jongkind is Academic Vice Principal of Tyndale House, Cambridge, where he leads the Greek New Testament research project. He teaches in the Faculty of Divinity of the University of Cambridge and is a Fellow of St Edmund's College.

His academic work involves studying manuscripts of the Greek New Testament and the differences in wording between them. Through Tyndale House, his roles within the university, and various mentoring initiatives in and around Cambridge over many years, he has been closely involved in the lives of many academics of diverse disciplines. He is a proud father and grandfather, and loves the outside.

GROWING IN UNDERSTANDING

GROWING IN UNDERSTANDING

Devotions for Christian academics

Dirk Jongkind

Apollos

First published in Great Britain in 2025

Apollos
Studio 101, The Record Hall, 16–16A Baldwin's Gardens, London EC1N 7RJ
https://ivpbooks.com

EU GPSR Authorised Representative
LOGOS EUROPE, 9 rue Nicolas Poussin, 17000, La Rochelle, France
Email: Contact@logoseurope.eu

British Library Cataloguing-in-Publication Data
A catalogue record for this book is available from the British Library

ISBN 978-1-78974-581-8
eBook ISBN 978-1-78974-582-5

1 3 5 7 9 10 8 6 4 2

Typeset by Fakenham Prepress Solutions, Fakenham, Norfolk NR21 8NL
First printed in Great Britain by Clays Ltd

eBook by Fakenham Prepress Solutions, Fakenham, Norfolk NR21 8NL

Produced on paper from sustainable sources

Inter-Varsity Press publishes Christian books that are true to the Bible and that communicate the gospel, develop discipleship and strengthen the church for its mission in the world.

IVP originated within the Inter-Varsity Fellowship, now the Universities and Colleges Christian Fellowship, a student movement connecting Christian Unions in universities and colleges throughout Great Britain, and a member movement of the International Fellowship of Evangelical Students. Website: www.uccf.org.uk. That historic association is maintained, and all senior IVP staff and committee members subscribe to the UCCF Basis of Faith.

Contents

Introduction

This book is for Christians in the academy. It is for scholars and scientists, for students and their teachers. I wrote it to encourage those of us who work in an academic context to read the Bible better.

The academic world consists largely of three groups of people: students, paid and unpaid researchers and faculty. The boundaries between the groups are not always clear, but the distinction will do for our purposes. Students have come to learn, and especially once they embark on a master's or higher degree they have a strong desire to learn. If you are pursuing a degree with an M in the title, you are part of that vibrant community of people who form the heart of the collective project designed to enhance and deepen our knowledge of reality. This project is the academy.

Some of us will have landed full-time research positions, either working towards a doctorate or as a post-doc involved in an academic project. You may be involved in the stressful business of hopping from a short contract to the next post-doc and always on the lookout for something permanent that offers a bit more security than you currently have. And then there are faculty: people responsible for teaching and providing leadership and, hopefully, able to do actual research besides writing funding applications and drowning in administration.

All three groups are part of the academic life. Our particular worries and responsibilities may differ, but what we have in common is that we have made the life of the mind the focus of our pursuits. We have the desire, the ability and the opportunity to spend this season of our life in the academy. Some may prefer me to make a distinction between scholars and scientists, but allow me to use the word 'scholar', as it is also used in that academic good-news word 'scholarship', where it means that someone else is paying for our studies.

A special word for those doing master's courses in a theological training college or seminary. It may be that you will benefit from this book more than anyone else. All of us run into the problem that on occasion we are too much affected by discipline-specific problems. For those who are studying Scripture (and much more) on an almost full-time basis, it is guaranteed that you will face struggles. I hope that you will find some comfort in reading how the words of the Bible also speak to the process of learning and the life of the mind.

If you are a Christian academic in the widest possible sense, this book is for you. It has been written to encourage you to read the Bible as an academic. It is written to help you understand yourself and some of your occupational hazards better. We serve God with our minds on a daily basis. Let us read Scripture with the same rigour and sharpness of mind that is the bread and butter of our disciplines.

The separate chapters of this book are more or less distinct units without strict organisation. This has been done on purpose, following the model of the book of Proverbs. The self-proclaimed purpose of that biblical book is to make us wise. For large sections (chapters 10–30) Proverbs divulges its wisdom without a clear underlying structure. We need to read Scripture as scholars in order to live wisely in the academy. A hierarchical organisation of the material might hinder rather than achieve this purpose.

This book can be used in academic fellowship groups (Christian graduate unions, faculty prayer groups, etc.) to freshen up our Bible reading; sometimes it is good to listen to an outside voice. At the same time, there are many Christians who work in relative isolation. This was at the forefront of my mind when I put the material together. Whether you use this book individually or as part of a fellowship group, I have added some questions for reflection at the end of each chapter.

The Scripture passages are important. Often only a few phrases within a single sentence are unpacked. Acquiring the Bible's wisdom means meditating on the Bible's words. The things I have written about the passage are not half as interesting as the words from Scripture themselves. At the same time, I am aware that I have tried to cram a lot into a relatively short space and owe you a (half-hearted) apology for that.

This book is dedicated to Bruce Winter, former Warden of Tyndale House, who took me (and many others) under his wing and mentored me when I was a young, often clueless, academic. His personal investment has helped me to see more of Christ.

Academic life is not always easy

Jeremiah 20:7–18

[7]O LORD, you have deceived me,
  and I was deceived;
you are stronger than I,
  and you have prevailed.
I have become a laughingstock all the day;
  everyone mocks me.
[8]For whenever I speak, I cry out,
  I shout, 'Violence and destruction!'
For the word of the LORD has become for me
  a reproach and derision all day long.
[9]If I say, 'I will not mention him,
  or speak any more in his name',
there is in my heart as it were a burning fire
  shut up in my bones,
and I am weary with holding it in,
  and I cannot.
[10]For I hear many whispering.
  Terror is on every side!
'Denounce him! Let us denounce him!'
  say all my close friends,
  watching for my fall.
'Perhaps he will be deceived;
  then we can overcome him
  and take our revenge on him.'
[11]But the LORD is with me as a dread warrior;
  therefore my persecutors will stumble;

they will not overcome me.
They will be greatly shamed,
for they will not succeed.
Their eternal dishonour
will never be forgotten.
12O LORD of hosts, who tests the righteous,
who sees the heart and the mind,
let me see your vengeance upon them,
for to you have I committed my cause.
13Sing to the LORD;
praise the LORD!
For he has delivered the life of the needy
from the hand of evildoers.
14Cursed be the day
on which I was born!
The day when my mother bore me,
let it not be blessed!
15Cursed be the man who brought the news to my father,
'A son is born to you',
making him very glad.
16Let that man be like the cities
that the LORD overthrew without pity;
let him hear a cry in the morning
and an alarm at noon,
17because he did not kill me in the womb;
so my mother would have been my grave,
and her womb forever great.
18Why did I come out from the womb
to see toil and sorrow,
and spend my days in shame?

'Cursed be the day on which I was born!'

We are not starting at the happiest of places in reading Jeremiah 20. The language Jeremiah uses is harsh, there is little hope, and a phrase such as 'Cursed be the day on which I was born!' is, hopefully, not something we would echo. But these words are in the Bible. So there is good reason to take them seriously. And since we do not want to avoid the difficult issues, it may be good to get real from the outset: life is not always easy.

This passage is one of those autobiographical passages that occur regularly in the book of Jeremiah, in which the prophet seems to argue with God, asking questions and complaining about this or that (normally about his audience or how they treat him). The frankness of Jeremiah's response to God is remarkable and may make us even somewhat uncomfortable – as may this passage being part of the inspired and canonical Scriptures. What are we going to do with these words from Jeremiah?

The fact that the nature of Jeremiah's complaint concerns the task God had given him and the great personal cost he faces in fulfilling his ministry will help us to understand this passage. And this personal cost is expressed in dark tones: 'Cursed be the day on which I was born!' Still, Jeremiah was a true servant of God and his grumblings give us a unique insight into the inner life of this long-serving prophet, a prophet whose ministry played out over many decades and ended only after a substantial part of the nation had been carried away into exile after a terrible siege.

So what have we read? Verses 7 to 12 are an okayish section. Admittedly, verse 7 sounds somewhat dubious: how can you say to God that he deceived you, that he duped you? However, the next verse gives us a reason for this strong statement: it is his message that has caused Jeremiah to be a laughing stock. The messenger is derided and despised because his message goes against the concerns of contemporary society.

It gets better in verse 9, where there are some good devotional thoughts. Jeremiah cannot hold God's word inside himself: it has to be spoken. He cannot keep it in, even though close friends are watching for Jeremiah to fall, to be caught out in his words (verse 10). This situation is so dire that Jeremiah can only call out about his situation, 'Terror is on every side!' People are looking to take their revenge on Jeremiah. Still, verse 11 is a good triumphant verse – 'they will not overcome me' – and verse 12 is something we all hope for but dare not say: 'let me see your vengeance upon [my enemies]'.

Verse 13, a paragraph in itself, is outright jubilant and would not look out of place, for example, in Mary's famous song of praise in Luke 1, when she visits Elisabeth, who is also pregnant. It would make a fitting conclusion to this chapter as well. Jeremiah starts with pouring out his complaint before the Lord and then finishes with a restored trust in God's deliverance – it may lead us to think that all's well that ends well.

But then, from verse 14 onwards, Jeremiah seems to lose the plot. No longer a devout religious person, he descends into some serious and over-the-top self-pity: 'Cursed be the day on which I was born!' 'Cursed be the man who brought the news to my father.' He would have been better off stillborn. Jeremiah ends this chapter in misery, and we would have loved to see this misery resolved. After all, the Bible is supposed to give us comfort. It may be for this reason that it has been suggested that verse 13 originally came after verse 18 but by some kind of untraceable incident ended up at its current location. I wonder, though, what miserable scribe would have made such a change.

So what are we going to do with this passage? The first option, the most popular one, is that we do absolutely nothing with this text. It is in the Bible, buried deeply in the Old Testament, and we should just accept it as one of many curiosities: read and forget, and move on. A second option is to see this passage as reflecting an unhealthy mental condition. If a student at college, in a tutorial or seminar, or even a one-to-one conversation, were to utter something similar to what Jeremiah expresses in this chapter, I would send them immediately to the university counselling service. This student wouldn't be alone. Between 10 per cent and 20 per cent of all students need some sort of counselling during their studies.[1] But, at this stage, I am not yet prepared to go down this route with Jeremiah; it is too easy to ascribe a psychological problem to the prophet. So what is left as our third option is to try and understand what Jeremiah is saying in the context of the book. And it turns out, there is a lot of helpful context.

First of all, Jeremiah's troubles all happen because of his prophecies. When Jeremiah cries out, 'Terror is on every side!', he uses the same words to describe his own misery

1 In a well-resourced university such as Oxford the number of students seeking help just from the university's counselling service was 12.4 per cent for the year 2022–23 (https://www.ox.ac.uk/students/news/2024-02-19-student-welfare-and-support-services-reports-show-demand-remained-high-2022-23).

as he had used to describe the judgement on Pashhur, the temple official who had locked him up for the day (20:1–4). Jeremiah experiences the judgement himself.

Second, you may have picked up on how 20:14–18 reflects the language of Job in chapter 3, who also curses the day he was born. Apart from using the same language, I am not sure that there is any link. Perhaps more importantly, verse 18 ('Why did I come out of the womb ...?') is a clear reference back to the words of Jeremiah's own initial calling in Jeremiah 1:5:

> 'Before I formed you in the womb I knew you,
> and before you were born I consecrated you;
> I appointed you a prophet to the nations.'

Jeremiah wished he had never been born. The judgement he pronounces to the nation seems to rebound on him personally. His calling and his ministry are dire. There are further references to Jeremiah's calling. In 20:7–10, where Jeremiah laments the strength of those opposing him, reflect on what God had told him in 1:19: 'They will fight against you, but they shall not prevail against you, for I am with you, declares the Lord, to deliver you.'

All this does not change the force of the language Jeremiah is using, but it gives us some context. In our passage Jeremiah is crying out that the practical outcome of his ministry, as far as it concerns his own life and experience, is one of great personal hardship. Of course, as a prophet, as someone who trusts the Lord, he is able to see ahead and praise God for his prophetic deliverance from all evildoers; but, looking at his own day-to-day toil, the opposition he faces, how little fun it is do what he has to do, he cannot see anything but utter misery as he continues to preach the ultimate destruction of Jerusalem to a people who will not listen and will not repent. Rather than trying to resolve the tension by rearranging these verses, it is perhaps more realistic to leave the passage as it is and to accept the reality of Jeremiah's experience, an experience in which he prefigured the Man of Sorrows in a unique way.

So is there a lesson for us? The first one is this: doing God's work, preaching (as in the case of Jeremiah) or whatever we are called to do, is not always fun (#understatement). In practical terms, doing your research and going through the tedious process of gathering yet more data is often not what you want to do at the start of the day. It can be sheer misery; sometimes research is boring and it may include feeling quite lonely at some stage.

Some of us may be in the academy because we hope to make a good career out of it and to pay the bills; others are here because we are called to it. And following your calling is not always one big party. On the contrary, it may seem that we have been lured into a process that is less attractive on the inside than it looks from the outside. There is more romance in a PhD programme when you are not enrolled in one. We find ourselves doing serious research and wondering how we ended up doing this. We have always loved studying and seem to have a natural ability to do something 'intelligent', but now when it comes to the nuts and bolts of doing a higher degree, it sometimes turns out to be a rather dispiriting experience. At times it feels as though we have been duped into doing this, not least because there isn't anything of a realistic job prospect afterwards. It is a rather grim outlook.

Part of the problem is that we all know the idealised image of the 'successful' Christian. This is someone who goes from success to success, from publication to publication, from fame to ever greater fame. They can preach, they have sorted out their personal problems, and the only troubles they face are those that make for great sermon illustrations. And we think that we must model ourselves on them, with their influence and place at the table, as voices to be reckoned with and having earned the respect of society.

All this leaves us with the question: what do we think is the reality of true Christian obedience? Is it the golden image set up by Christian pop culture or is it the somewhat raw image of serving, being faithful, questioning ourselves, knowing that God will deliver, yet struggling on from day to day, while carrying a death sentence, a cross? Jeremiah suggests the latter, and he has written this for our consolation so that we might have hope. We are not alone. There is someone in heaven who calls us his brother, his sister, who has faced that same struggle of obedience. And he understands our complaints. He understands the outpouring of our hearts.

And then there is also a whole community of fellow strugglers. Not a group of people who are necessarily of a gloomy or depressed disposition but a group of brothers and sisters in Christ who know both sides of the equation: the doubt and difficulties, as well as the God who is faithful throughout.

Sing to the Lord;
  praise the Lord!
For he has delivered the life of the needy
  from the hand of evildoers.

For further reflection

1. In what ways have you been disappointed by the academic life? What are the things that have come as an unpleasant surprise?
2. Why do Christians often feel guilty when bringing their complaints before God?
3. What is the difference between knowing the standard to live up to and pretending to live up to that standard? How does Jeremiah 20 confront the idealised Christian life?

What community means

1 Thessalonians 2:1–12

1For you yourselves know, brothers, that our coming to you was not in vain. 2But though we had already suffered and been shamefully treated at Philippi, as you know, we had boldness in our God to declare to you the gospel of God in the midst of much conflict. 3For our appeal does not spring from error or impurity or any attempt to deceive, 4but just as we have been approved by God to be entrusted with the gospel, so we speak, not to please man, but to please God who tests our hearts. 5For we never came with words of flattery, as you know, nor with a pretext for greed – God is witness. 6Nor did we seek glory from people, whether from you or from others, though we could have made demands as apostles of Christ. 7But we were gentle among you, like a nursing mother taking care of her own children. 8So, being affectionately desirous of you, we were ready to share with you not only the gospel of God but also our own selves, because you had become very dear to us.

9For you remember, brothers, our labour and toil: we worked night and day, that we might not be a burden to any of you, while we proclaimed to you the gospel of God. 10You are witnesses, and God also, how holy and righteous and blameless was our conduct toward you believers. 11For you know how, like a father with his children, 12we exhorted each one of you and encouraged you and charged you to walk in a manner worthy of God, who calls you into his own kingdom and glory.

'For you yourselves know ...'

A large part of education is about the formation of the individual. Though there is a time and place for group assessments, in the end the individual student is the one who receives the degree. We will assess a student's progress, their response to the material offered in their degree, and we hope that the final classification is a fair reflection of their achievements. Writing a dissertation is a solitary process and the candidate must declare that it is all their own original work. And when that is completed, they have to start the loneliest exercise of all: the job-application process. It shouldn't therefore surprise us that isolation and loneliness are widespread among academics. The second chapter of 1 Thessalonians is very useful when thinking about notions of fellowship and community, things that are the direct opposite of isolation.

A phrase that stands out in this passage is found in 2:1: 'For you yourselves know'. Remarks such as 'you all know' or 'you will remember that' can function in a variety of ways. First, there is the 'unfriendly' mode: you are the audience, say, of mainly graduate scientists; I am the guest lecturer, whose sole purpose is to emphasise the gap of learnedness between you and me. I pontificate with 'I'd like to remind you, as without doubt you all know, Paul Ricoeur's treatment of the nature of testimony validates the whole discipline of theology.' Here the phrase 'you all know' serves to highlight your ignorance in contrast to my superior knowledge.[1]

1 Incidentally, Paul Ricoeur is a French philosopher of religion who wrote an essay on 'The Hermeneutics of Testimony', in which he may have argued something like this, but please don't judge me on my lack of understanding of Ricoeur – this is just a hypothetical example.

A friendlier use of 'you all know' conveys knowledge while trying to avoid the embarrassment of ignorance on the side of your listeners: 'You will all remember that this afternoon we meet at 3 p.m. to discuss the set text for the week.' A third way in which this phrase can be used is the most obvious one: a lecturer or speaker uses it simply because the audience does know, and this shared knowledge is relevant to a specific point. In our passage we have:

- For you yourselves know … (2:1);
- … as you know … (2:2);
- … as you know … (2:5);
- For you remember … (2:9);
- You are witnesses, and God also … (2:10);
- For you know … (2:11).

The sheer frequency of these phrases directs us to a particular point: that Paul and his audience share a common history and that Paul's behaviour exemplified a value he wants to get across. There is a specific way he wants to interact with the church.

Unlike the original readers, we as readers of this old text do not share their experience of knowing how Paul behaved among the young believers in Thessalonica. Thankfully though, as he reminds his first audience he informs us at the same time.

So let's first have a look at how Paul describes his behaviour among the Thessalonians, and then see how wisdom can be gained. In 2:2 Paul refers to the events that happened immediately before he arrived in the city. In the book of Acts we read about Paul's imprisonment in Philippi and how he had made use of his Roman citizenship to squeeze out an apology from the city magistrates (Acts 16). He still had to leave the city, but this negative experience is no excuse to be slack in the preaching of the word. On the contrary (2:3), he is confident of his message because he does not preach from false motives (2:3) and he has been approved by God to be entrusted with the gospel in order to please God, who tests Paul's heart (2:4).

Paul has a clear sense of God's activity in history: God is responsible for the message and for giving Paul this particular task and is the one who tests Paul as to his motives for doing what he does. Paul is not seeking glory from others (2:6). Of course this goes hand in hand with an awareness of living before God but still, in practice, a good many people try to do both, to live for God and to seek glory from others at the same time. However, Paul presents himself not just as being uninterested in human glory. He brings some evidence to the table, having actively abstained from the rights of an apostle, behaved as a mother taking care of her own children (2:7) and shared not only the gospel but also himself (2:8).

Paul was not afraid of working hard (2:9). Working night and day is a strong commitment and unlikely to be an exaggeration. After all, those to whom he has written remember very well how Paul behaved among them. He then throws in another family metaphor, namely that he exhorted the Thessalonians as a father to walk in a manner worthy of God, having set an example in his own life (2:11).

None of us has a similar calling to Paul's. We do not have the same personal commission to be an apostle or to instruct the church with apostolic authority. Nor do we have the visions he had. However, we have a calling as scholars and students, who are leading or who will lead others and want to do so wisely. There are aspects of Paul's experience with which we can identify. As for Paul, previous disappointment is no reason to become slack in our academic rigour, boldness or faithfulness. And, likewise, confidence in our academic ministry should be marked by not living our lives as academics from false motives but rather by being honest with colleagues and other students. We have been approved by God to be endowed with a level of intelligence, over which we have had very little influence; it is up to us to use this gift. We should use it to please God, because he tests our heart: you can fool close friends, you can fool your church, but you can't fool God.

The main point is perhaps the language Paul uses to describe his behaviour. He uses the paradigm of the family to explain the use of his apostolic gift: nurturing like a mother, exhorting like a father and addressing them as his siblings, his brothers and sisters. Not only does Paul show that he is secure in who he is, comparing himself to a nursing mother (elsewhere he even uses the language of labour pains), but he also demonstrates how people are to relate to one another. The various relationships within a functioning family are a model for what we can be to others.

A life based on Christian fellowship has much staying power. Think of yourself as a brother or a sister, a father, a family member of the people whom you can serve in your current work as a scholar. There are in academia different ways to interact with one another. Some are cold and standoffish, perhaps to cover up one's own vulnerabilities, while others may be based on being part of a jolly in-crowd that adopts a superior attitude to those who are outside.

But we can be different. Our discussions and our interactions, the way we relate to one another – and especially in the Christian context – can be modelled on the Christian paradigm we see in Paul. His confidence comes from God, and so can ours.

A family acknowledges diversity in character and in roles; we don't need to be uniform. How many of our colleagues will be surprised when we relate to them as family, without the need to keep up the unreal appearances often modelled by the academy? How will this change our conversations when we try to help and learn, when we choose to be together because we have that divine confidence without the need to earn respect by playing the prestige game? Family relations can be denied but they cannot be undone.

For further reflection

1 Some academics prefer solitude over company. What are the dangers of this attitude?
2 How would you describe the ideal community, where you feel both safe and warmly comfortable, but also intellectually stimulated? Have you ever experienced this?
3 How does Paul's manner of relating to the Thessalonians as a family member help us to understand and evaluate our own relationship with our physical families (even though these are often far from ideal)?

About receiving a position

Galatians 1:1–5

[1]Paul, an apostle – not from men nor through man, but
through Jesus Christ and God the Father, who raised him
from the dead – [2]and all the brothers who are with me,
To the churches of Galatia:
[3]Grace to you and peace from God our Father and the
Lord Jesus Christ, [4]who gave himself for our sins to deliver
us from the present evil age, according to the will of our God
and Father, [5]to whom be the glory forever and ever. Amen.

Not … through man

A big risk when reading the Bible is to underestimate the depth and deliberate precision of much of its language. Every single phrase is there for a reason. And from the very start of this letter the precise form of the language is important. In the first sentence Paul uses a standard linguistic device that draws attention to a positive statement by negating its apparent opposite: 'an apostle – *not* from men *nor* through man, *but* through …' – two denials followed by a positive affirmation.

As becomes abundantly clear in the course of this letter, Paul claims that his apostleship is rooted in a divine appointment. And he underlines this with a double denial: 'not from men' refers to the idea that an apostle, as the word *apostolos* makes clear, is someone who has been sent. Paul has not been sent as an ambassador from people nor, as 'through man' signifies, which is in the singular with reference to the category 'humanity', was he appointed in his role by a human being or through human agency. When Paul starts by saying that he was neither sent by men nor appointed by man he is guiding our expectations so that what follows will be seen as a natural contrast: 'but through Jesus Christ and God the Father'. Though only the second of the two denials is turned around into a positive (namely the 'not *through* man'), we are left to conclude that the positive version of the first denial is also intended, that is, not from men but from Jesus Christ and God the Father. Still, it is the second of the denials that is positively countered: 'not … through man, but through Jesus Christ and God the Father'. Of course it is obvious that the term 'God the Father' forms an appropriate contrast to 'not … through man', God and man clearly being on different levels. But the inclusion of 'Jesus Christ' here tells us a lot about how Paul thinks about the parentage of Jesus. Appointment by Jesus Christ can be appropriately contrasted with appointment by man, for Jesus is God.

Jesus Christ and God the Father are the ones who put Paul in his role as apostle, and it is their authority he is representing. In the remainder of this letter it becomes clear how important this divine origin of Paul's apostleship was for Paul, as it should be for the churches he is writing to.

There is a more general truth here. It is reassuring to see someone who has confidence because they know they have been appointed by Jesus Christ and God the Father. Elsewhere Paul labels himself a called apostle. He finds his confidence in the authority and the person of who called and appointed him into his role.

I have noticed in Cambridge that there is at every level in the academic structure a lot of uncertainty about people's right to be here, a sense of insecurity fed by a system that tells us, 'What are you doing here? Are you good enough to be here? Be careful because sooner or later someone is going to find you out and expose you for the fraud you actually are.'[1] In general, people outside North America are not particularly good at affirming people, and many academic institutions in Europe have a knack of encouraging any sliver of self-doubt and of feeding that existential angst of not really making the mark. Of course those who survive this onslaught are either those who are truly brilliant or who have become unhealthily arrogant. Yet, if these are the main options for how to live and study in academia, we are in a sorry state.

Re-enter Paul. His appointment as apostle was not by mankind but by God the Father and by Jesus Christ the Son, and Paul knew it. Not only did this give him authority; it also gave him confidence. A called apostle. And here is a valuable lesson for us. Into what role has God called you? What is your calling? I readily admit that Paul's calling came with a lot of external confirmation, and it is unlikely that our own calling came with similar signs. I have seen the light many times but never like Paul on the road to Damascus. Still, we each have our own calling in life. It may be, at this season of our life, to produce the best possible PhD we can, in the most disciplined and efficient way possible, within our particular context; or it may be to finish our current research project or to teach the students who have been entrusted to

1 Imposter syndrome is rife in the academic world, as many discussions on Reddit confirm (e.g. r/AskAcademia or r/PhD). The *Times Higher Education* ran a short article offering the best secular advice ('When am I going to be found out? Tackling academic impostor syndrome', 1 December 2022, https://www.timeshighereducation.com/campus/when-am-i-going-be-found-out-tackling-academic-impostor-syndrome).

us. We have to take our present circumstances seriously as our current calling. God's call is not something that lies in the future: it is for now. Do not worry what your calling or role will be in two or four years; just make sure that you have today sorted out.

Once we realise that our current position is the place where God wants us to be faithful, we can reach a place where our confidence and sense of affirmation no longer depend on those around us or on the praise of our colleagues or supervisor. Our confidence is no longer even dependent on our sense of self-worth. Instead, we find our affirmation in realising that we can say Paul's words after him: 'I am a scholar, not because man made me a scholar but because God appointed me' or 'I am a PhD student not because I am clever or because someone encouraged me to do a PhD, but because I find my confidence in God having appointed me to this position'. Being aware of our calling is not the same as formulating our career goals. It has everything to do with discharging the responsibility and task we find ourselves in at this moment. And then we can say with Paul: 'not from men nor through man, but through Jesus Christ and God the Father'. That should give us sufficient confidence to live our lives before him, to study, to research or to think well today, for God's glory.

For further reflection

1 Every positive trait can easily descend into something that is wrong. Confidence can turn into arrogance, while knowing your own inadequacy can turn into debilitating uncertainty. How can you apply divine confidence to your life in a healthy way, avoiding all the pitfalls?

2. Imposter syndrome is real in the academy, in part because one cannot be good at everything. How do we help other Christians in the academy?
3. And what would we say to our non-Christian colleagues? How can we speak to them about our identity, placement and calling in Christ?

God's personalised comfort

Jeremiah 45

1The word that Jeremiah the prophet spoke to Baruch, the
son of Neriah, when he wrote these words in a book at the
dictation of Jeremiah, in the fourth year of Jehoiakim the
son of Josiah, king of Judah: 2'Thus says the LORD, the God
of Israel, to you, O Baruch: 3You said, 'Woe is me! For the
LORD has added sorrow to my pain. I am weary with my
groaning, and I find no rest.' 4Thus shall you say to him,
Thus says the LORD: Behold, what I have built I am breaking
down, and what I have planted I am plucking up – that is,
the whole land. 5And do you seek great things for yourself?
Seek them not, for behold, I am bringing disaster upon all
flesh, declares the LORD. But I will give you your life as a
prize of war in all places to which you may go.'

Seeking great things for yourself

After I had moved to another country to continue my studies, someone took me under his wing and became a mentor to me. His name is Bruce Winter, and he was then the head (a position quaintly called 'warden') of Tyndale House, Cambridge.[1] I owe him a lot, not least because he taught me that Scripture has a specific and direct application to those of us who spend time in the academy. Bruce Winter used to cite the words from verse 5 quite often: 'do you seek great things for yourself? Seek them not.' They are good

1 Tyndale House, Cambridge, my current employer, is a residential research centre for biblical studies and is used by many graduate and postgraduate researchers in the field.

words, even though they need to be understood in context. I have never forgotten Bruce's words, though I have been guilty more than once of forgetting their message.

Jeremiah 45 is a short chapter and it is set in an important period, the fourth year of Jehoiakim's reign. It is the year when the king of Babylon, Nebuchadnezzar, who has just taken the crown (Jeremiah 25:1), takes the first captives to Babylon, among whom is Daniel (Daniel 1:1–2). The nation of Judah is allowed to continue its existence and the Temple has not yet been destroyed (that was not to take place until eighteen years later: 2 Kings 25:8–9). This fourth year of Jehoiakim has already figured twice in the book of Jeremiah. The first was in Jeremiah 25, among a number of chronological references, including the announcement that the servitude in Babylon would last seventy years (25:11). Also, after twenty-three years of Jeremiah's ministry, it becomes increasingly clear that the nation as a whole is doomed (25:3).

The second reference to the fourth year of Jehoiakim occurs in Jeremiah 36:1, where Jeremiah is commanded by the Lord to take a scroll and write everything down that God has spoken through Jeremiah. This event triggers the prophecy dictated by Jeremiah that the scribe Baruch has to write down (36:4). Baruch is told that, since Jeremiah has a restraining order for the Temple, he has to read the book publicly in the temple (36:5–6), which he does in the fifth year of Jehoiakim (36:9–10). The task of writing the scroll is definitely easier than reading it for everyone to hear. To tell people that they will serve Babylon, that the city will be destroyed and that God's judgement is coming involves pressure and public exposure. And we all know the story of how the king eventually burns this book bit by bit (36:20–24) and fails to take heed of the prophecy. It is perfectly understandable that Baruch does not look forward to doing this. His position is already tied up with Jeremiah's, and he now has to become the public face of Jeremiah's ministry.

So it is at this particular juncture, when Baruch has been told to write at Jeremiah's dictation and to broadcast God's judgement on the nation, that God sends Baruch a personal message of encouragement – because God equips and encourages his servants for the tasks they have been given.

So what is God's message to Baruch in Jeremiah 45? First, God knows Baruch's anguish, he even cites his own words back to him: 'You said …' (45:3). While we do not read anything about how Baruch felt about his assignment, it appears that he had a very understandable reaction: 'Woe is me! For the LORD has added sorrow to my pain. I am weary.' It is not just a modern phenomenon that people feel tired and exhausted from constant pressure and anxiety. Baruch felt the same and lamented his role in the proclamation of God's judgement.

Second, God communicates to Baruch through Jeremiah, which was God's normal way of communication in Baruch's days: 'The word that Jeremiah the prophet spoke to Baruch' (45:1). God could have spoken to Baruch directly but instead does not use any extraordinary means.

Third, in 45:4 God explains the times in a message that is intended as a personal encouragement. Baruch's life is put in the context of the big things that will happen to the nation. The nation is going to lose its independent existence, the Temple will be destroyed in the near future and thousands of people will lose their lives. Baruch is reminded of the wider context in which he lives: judgement is about to happen.

Fourth, only now does God tell Baruch to check his ambitions. In the context of the impending disaster, Baruch is told not to 'seek great things for yourself': they are not going to happen. What are these great things that Baruch might have been seeking? We are not told, but I can imagine a few. Revival, for example: an unprecedented conversion following his reading of God's message. Or a miraculous turn in Baruch's mental distress and anxiety: perhaps a sudden injection of supernatural boldness and confidence. Or a way (for example, losing his voice) for Baruch to avoid the upcoming public reading of the message of doom. But whatever it was, God simply says, 'do you seek great things for yourself? Seek them not': judgement is going to take place.

So where is the encouragement? There have been few positives so far, apart from God indicating that he sees and knows Baruch's groaning. The answer is that, for executing his task faithfully, Baruch will receive his life as a prize of war wherever he goes. He will keep his life (Hebrew *nephesh*) or, perhaps better, he will keep his soul. 'Do you seek great things for yourself? Seek them not', for what benefit is it to win the whole world and lose your soul (Matthew 16:26)?

Each of these points can be reflected in the life of a Christian academic. You may, like me, be a bit of a dreamer hoping to save the world, to be the Bruce Willis of scholarship, the Tom Cruise of Christianity or perhaps the Taylor Swift of evangelicalism. We may dream of great things being written about us. Well, God's message to Baruch checks our bravado fantasies. God knows us, he made us and he has something to say to us.

First, God knows our desperation, our sense of inadequacy when we face tasks that fill us with dread. We may say, 'God, why do you add sorrow to my pain?' Yet God knows and even talks to us, and he does so usually in the way he normally communicates. In our day this is through Scripture, through reflection and through our brothers and sisters around us in the community of believers. And he wants us to understand the bigger narrative of our times and our situation. Jesus has given us an extensive description of the main characteristics of our context between his ascension and return. And though, thankfully, he is in control and is gathering his people from across the whole earth, the earth itself remains hostile to him and to the gospel. Expect hardships. It may be that you are experiencing a period of political stability or your institution seems quiet, unlike the turmoil Baruch is facing. Such times are a blessing but do not take them for granted. The temptation to waste these in complacency is often strong. We may want to rule when it is not yet time for the church to do so. Therefore, even in seemingly quiet times, take Jesus's analysis of the state of the world we live in seriously.

So, given our situation, what will happen if we seek great things for ourselves? I have seen people set their hearts on self-centred goals – a great position, a promising career, a solid reputation – and they may have won the world but lost their soul. Our word from Jeremiah is crystal clear and expressed in a simple imperative: do not seek great things for yourself.

Like too many Christian academics, if we play the social game of seeking prestige for too long, we will lose at some point. If we lose sight of God's objectives and replace them with the norms of secular success, we will lose more than the Christian commitment we started out with: we will lose our life.

Baruch received this personal prophecy in the fourth year of Jehoiakim, when he was writing down the book of the prophecies of Jeremiah at his dictation. We do not know how long it took to finish that work or if there was some other delay before Baruch stood up in the ninth month of the fifth year and started reading out the condemnation of the nation (36:9–10). Did Baruch need to overcome his pain and sorrow in the intervening period? Or was this the first great opportunity for a public reading of God's word? We don't know. We have only part of the story. But we do know that the scribe was a scholar named Baruch, who at one point was told to give a public account of the text he had been painstakingly recording for so long. And he went into the fight with a promise.

We can take heart from that promise given to Baruch that God will grant him his life wherever he went. Our Lord has given us eternal life that no one can take away. No one can pluck us out of his hand, and therefore we persevere in the midst of our pain and sorrow, filled with an inexplicable joy that will last for ever.

For further reflection

1 Sometimes we are in survival mode and simply try to get through the next term or semester. But then we get an opportunity that asks us to step out boldly for the gospel. How have you dealt with it in the past? What has been your greatest failing and what has been a blessing?

2 How is it a comfort that God quotes back to Baruch what he has been saying?
3 How can we distinguish between healthy and unhealthy personal ambition?

To become wise I: Where to begin

Proverbs 1:1–7

1The proverbs of Solomon, son of David, king of Israel:
2To know wisdom and instruction,
to understand words of insight,
3to receive instruction in wise dealing,
in righteousness, justice, and equity;
4to give prudence to the simple,
knowledge and discretion to the youth –
5Let the wise hear and increase in learning,
and the one who understands obtain guidance,
6to understand a proverb and a saying,
the words of the wise and their riddles.
7The fear of the LORD is the beginning of knowledge;
fools despise wisdom and instruction.

The beginning of knowledge

Higher education is, in part, about the intellectual life, about learning, problem solving and constructing an argument. We aim to increase the pool of knowledge, perhaps even to become an authority in our field. And as such we may resonate with the opening of the book of Proverbs: 'to know wisdom and instruction'. At first sight, Solomon seems to be on our side as he gives us a magnificent description of what the professional pursuits of the believing academic could look like.

The text proper starts off with four infinitives in 1:2–4. The first three are from the perspective of the hearer, 'to know', 'to understand', 'to receive', with the second of these repeated in 1:6.

In 1:4, the point of view changes from the hearer to the speaker with the verb 'to give' instead of something that is received by the reader. At this point the intended audience is mentioned: 'the simple' and 'the youth'. Normally the older we get the more we increase in wisdom, or at least that is what is supposed to happen. 'Simple' is used in the sense of being untrained in wisdom. The term 'youth' is equally important, as it explains the shape of the first nine chapters of Proverbs. In these chapters wisdom is cast in the form of parents talking to their son, in 1:8–9; 2:1; 3:1; 4:1; 4:10; and so on. The parents speak in short speeches and not until chapter 10 do we get the familiar collection of short two- and three-line proverbs. But even that section starts deliberately with 10:1: 'A wise son makes a glad father, but a foolish son is a sorrow to his mother.' The son is mentioned at the head of these individual sayings just to continue the pattern set in the previous chapters.

Though the early chapters of Proverbs are couched in terms of a parent speaking to a son, a wise person would do well not to limit the application of this book to young people. That is what 1:5 says: 'Let the wise hear and increase in learning, and the one who understands obtain guidance.' The wise person will benefit greatly from Proverbs, and the wise do need to continually pursue wisdom because life is often puzzling and perplexing. For example, in Proverbs 30:2 someone points out, 'Surely I am too stupid to be a man, I have not the understanding of a man.' The wise person needs guidance too, and intellectuals are no different.

Understanding the content of the book of Proverbs is not simple or straightforward, however. There is work to do to understand 'a proverb and a saying' (1:6). The word 'riddle' is used, and acquiring wisdom is not merely the communication of propositional truth. It includes pondering and reflecting on words. Deep truth is conveyed metaphorically, unlike the language of maths or physics. The wisdom of the wise is packed into riddles. Which means that speed reading is our greatest enemy. Perhaps most of our previous exposure to Proverbs has been through one of those plans to read through the Bible in a year. This works well for many parts of Scripture but not for Proverbs. Acquiring wisdom happens through slow thought and meditation, and so does the communication of wisdom.

Then we arrive at verse 7, an epistemological thunderclap: 'The fear of the LORD is the beginning of knowledge.' The word 'knowledge' is picked up again from verse 2, as in 'To know wisdom and instruction'. Also note that it says here 'the beginning of *knowledge*', not 'the beginning of wisdom' as it says later in 9:10 or in Psalm 111:10. Knowing has a foundation, which is the fear of the Lord.

We will leave aside the question how many clever people without any fear of the Lord still seem to know so much and sometimes even to possess deep and insightful knowledge. Here we simply take the positive case that is made to us, the people of God: 'The fear of the LORD is the beginning of knowledge.' What is this?

First, fear of the Lord means that we know our place in relation to God himself. We know enough of God's strength, power and overwhelming glory that we have a deep sense of awe, of appropriate fear towards someone who ranks infinitely higher than we do. But it is not just a sense of awe. When Jesus sends his disciples on a mission tour through

Israel he warns them not to be afraid of men (Matthew 10:26). And then he adds in Matthew 10:28: 'And do not fear those who kill the body but cannot kill the soul. Rather fear him who can destroy both soul and body in hell.' The expression 'fear of the LORD' does include the notion that our Father is also the one who will judge. As Paul says in 2 Corinthians 5:10–11, 'For we must all appear before the judgement seat of Christ, so that each one may receive what is due for what he has done in the body, whether good or evil. Therefore, *knowing the fear of the Lord*, we persuade others.' Fear of the Lord has a practical implication for when we hear his word. If someone of high rank speaks to us, we listen; we wouldn't dare do otherwise. Fear of the Lord means standing in the right relation to the Lord.

Second, fear of the Lord is the beginning of knowledge or, perhaps better, the beginning of all knowing. Because the assumption is that knowing always means having a relationship with. Knowledge as understood in Scripture is relational. Or, to put it negatively, knowledge is not neutral but has an effect on the one who knows. You cannot unsee the things you have seen; the neurological pathways have been formed. So how can we know without being contaminated? How can we become wise? And the answer is clear: we need to have a proper relationship to God, who is the only wise God (Romans 16:27).

Third, the fear of the Lord means something for how we want to approach our academic study. And this is true for both scholars and scientists. Our studies can only qualify as knowledge if we see our topic in the context of a right relationship with God. So let's consider biblical and theological studies. If this is your subject you have the privilege to study a field that has immediate eternity value. You are studying the details of how God has revealed himself, the vehicles (people or languages) he used. You are studying how these truths were received, how people have applied them in the past or how folk like the Puritans busied themselves trying to unravel the finer details of God's work in the human soul. All these things are true knowledge but only if you receive them in the fear of God and know about whom you are speaking. And, yes, knowledge should lead to wisdom, and the more knowledge you gather the more wisdom you need and the more you need the fear of the Lord.

To give another non-controversial example. People do not rise from the dead. There are dozens of biological reasons that militate against the possibility of this ever happening. However, our fear of the Lord puts these biological facts into a new and better context. We revel in every additional reason that our fellow biologists advance to prove their point because it only shows the magnificence of the God we fear, who also created biology, by the way. We know the God who has spoken and risen from the dead. We know the one who provides us with a bigger context. We know the fear of the Lord.

Doing research, trying to expand our understanding of reality, is slow and difficult work. So is acquiring wisdom. But, if we want to live well, it is good to set our heart on listening to him who is the source of all wisdom.

For further reflection

1. Do you have wise persons in your life? How do you think they became wise?
2. Do you ever take the time to ponder the words of

Scripture, either alone or in a group, without feeling the rush to move on to the next verse or to the next part of the evening? What is the value of quiet meditation on the wisdom of the Bible?

3 Wisdom is the skill of living well, and life consists of much more than the time we devote to church, fellowship and building up our faith. What is your experience in applying (or not applying) the wisdom of Scripture to all of life?

To become wise II: Seduction

Proverbs 1:8–19

8Hear, my son, your father's instruction,
and forsake not your mother's teaching,
9for they are a graceful garland for your head
and pendants for your neck.
10My son, if sinners entice you,
do not consent.
11If they say, 'Come with us, let us lie in wait for blood;
let us ambush the innocent without reason;
12like Sheol let us swallow them alive,
and whole, like those who go down to the pit;
13we shall find all precious goods,
we shall fill our houses with plunder;
14throw in your lot among us;
we will all have one purse' –
15my son, do not walk in the way with them;
hold back your foot from their paths,
16for their feet run to evil,
and they make haste to shed blood.
17For in vain is a net spread
in the sight of any bird,
18but these men lie in wait for their own blood;
they set an ambush for their own lives.
19Such are the ways of everyone who is greedy for unjust
gain;
it takes away the life of its possessors.

Do not do bad things with bad people

In the previous section we thought a little about that surprising starting point of the book of Proverbs, namely that a right attitude to God and a correct perception of him is the beginning of all knowledge. Unless you live in an epistemic world in which God exists, who is fearsome, who has spoken and who is active, you will always stay simple and act like a fool.

Proverbs has been given to instruct us, to make us wise, and it does so by giving us proverbs and sayings that do need reflection and serious thought because, as 1:7 also says, they are often put in the form of riddles.

Most of us will remember that Proverbs contains a number of distinct sections. The first nine chapters tend to be short speeches set in terms of a parent speaking to a son. These short speeches contain strong warnings, of which this passage is a clear example. And these warnings are given because, if the son ignores them, he will not live wisely but end up with a destroyed life.

The book of Proverbs does not deal in nuances: you are either a fool or on the path to wisdom; you are doing either the good thing or the bad. And the upshot of this is that it is possible to speak truth and wisdom without inflicting death by a thousand qualifications. So, in line with our general intent of reading the Bible for ourselves in the context of academia, I suggest that our passage helps us to think about the following question: why do people lose their faith during their postgraduate studies and possibly even as a result of their studies?

Our passage opens with a call to listen to the teaching of both the father and the mother (1:8). Following their wisdom is like jewellery, precious and attractive. But this positive note is then followed by two warnings. The first is a brief one in verse 10: 'if sinners entice you, do not consent' – do not be willing. This is then unpacked in the more elaborate version of the second warning: 'If they say …', 'do not walk in the way with them; hold back your foot from their paths' (1:11, 15).

What is it that they are saying that might be so attractive? Well, for starters these sinners have no problem taking life and possessions from a category of people they apparently deeply despise (1:11–12). And taking their possessions (1:13) is therefore no problem and helps these seducers to live the comfortable life they want. What is more, they offer to the son not just wealth and a good life but also membership of a group that will look after him: '"throw in your lot among us"' (1:14).

The parents have good reason to warn the son. Because their feet 'run to evil' and the shedding of blood (1:16), in the end it will be their own life and blood they are shedding (1:18): 'Such are the ways of everyone who is greedy for unjust gain; it takes away the life of its possessors' (1:19).

Something here should give us pause before we dive into any application. And that is the curious way in which the potential seduction is described: 'Come, let us do evil things, let us steal, let us kill, let us be horrible people together.' For most of us this is not a particularly attractive way of life. Why would we want to be a horrible person? Furthermore, we are still at the beginning of the book, so will the advice really be all this blunt and simplistic? 'Don't do bad things with bad people!' Who would need such an obvious warning? Where is the deep wisdom in this?

If we are not to conclude that Proverbs is a shallow book, we might try and give its wisdom the benefit of the doubt. We need to think again about the actual shape of the words that would turn the son into a bloodthirsty fool. As long as he shares the value system of his parents, from which this advice has arisen, the invitation to become a horrible person does not have much of a pull. But, to understand the riddles of the wise, what sort of words may be used to try and draw someone away from the faith and change the value system they were taught at home? What would be the subtle persuasion that we may not as easily recognise as being evil but that might lead us down the path of these sinners? Or, in terms of the question posed earlier, how might a Christian graduate student lose their faith? Let's listen in on how their thought process might develop.

'So, here we are, at the place of learning, the academy, with its ancient buildings, its collective intellectual tradition, its transformative power, and we are now a part of this world. And let's face it, I mean, facts are facts: we are probably a bit more intelligent than most Christians, right? After all, how many ordinary folk in the pew have ever done a bit of serious study of the things they believe? Most of them have not had the years of education we have enjoyed. It is absolutely the right thing that people make sacrifices so that we can study. Whether they give me a bit of respect for what I am achieving, or whether they pay their taxes diligently so that I can continue to do what I am here to do, it is just part of how things are. Moreover, the people in the church are giving for their own benefit because they pay for me so that I will be able to teach them all the things they had never thought of before. The life of an academic deserves to be rewarded adequately.'

And one way or another, our privileged Christian PhD student can very easily allow a sense of entitlement into their thinking, where their current position is right because they have earned their place by their own efforts. The first step in the seduction is to believe that you are entitled to be looked after, especially by those who have the means to do so, but also by those who have less.

Step two: 'Now that I am in the academy, I realise that there are people who are cleverer than I am. But, wait, they are interested in what I am doing: they listen to my ideas, they open up a place at the table and they treat me as if I were already a real intellectual. Yes, they do know much more than I do and they make me uncertain at times, but it is just a matter of sticking around before I am truly one of them. I can be an academic. I can lead the life I see them leading. I can throw in my lot with them. The academy will look after me if I could only worm my way in. It is a life I'd love to have.'

And this is the next step of the seduction. Our budding academic develops an unhealthy ambition and has changed their value system in the process. The faith once delivered to the saints is no longer their main ethical reality but has been replaced by what they now admire. What we admire and what we want to be drive our desires and become the main motivator for many of the smaller choices we make. What provides us now with the distinction between good and bad is the ambition to belong to a group we appreciate for what its members have achieved intellectually. We admire them and therefore ascribe a higher status to them and consider their views to have more authority than our own unenlightened opinions.

The power of the sociological seduction of the intellectual life is very strong and it is always there. I have noticed very often that undergraduates, master's and doctoral students, and many other groups started following strange doctrines not because they were set on following heresies or on bringing God's word into disrepute. No, they ended up doing it because they wanted to give up their old convictions when a new set of convictions was available to them, a new value system found in a class of people they had learned to admire deeply. And, once the focus of our esteem changes, lots of other things follow. We may adopt a new paradigm lock, stock and barrel. We may hold a particular opinion because it feels so natural and self-evident. And we forget that it is not our own well thought-through opinion but that of a group or supervisor we admire. Even though our new standpoint may sit poorly with the faith of the church, it sits very cosily in the value system of that intellectual life that now feels to us like a nice warm sweater. And the result is that the child ends up at the place they were warned against.

'The fear of the LORD is the beginning of knowledge' (1:7). This principle should drive our value system, not our membership of the sociological group we feel so at home with, not the values of those with such a dazzling intellect, not the ideas of those who can offer us a career we really, really want (deep down and without admitting it to anyone) – because the wisdom of this world, with all its shine and lustre, with all its phenomenal achievements, will perish and be shown to be foolishness if it is not based on the fear of the Lord.

'Such are the ways of everyone who is greedy for unjust gain; it takes away the life of its possessors' (1:19).

Beware of the seduction of the intellectual status, be aware that, as a follower of Christ, you are not owed the right to study but that he has called you to your studies in his grace and for his glory.

For further reflection

1. What powerful intellectual seductions have you seen in others' lives and in your own life?
2. What are the ways and strategies to avoid falling into the trap that has been set for you?
3. How can we help the generation coming after us?

To become wise III: The urgent need to chase wisdom

Proverbs 1:20–33

20Wisdom cries aloud in the street,
in the markets she raises her voice;
21at the head of the noisy streets she cries out;
at the entrance of the city gates she speaks:
22'How long, O simple ones, will you love being simple?
How long will scoffers delight in their scoffing
and fools hate knowledge?
23If you turn at my reproof,
behold, I will pour out my spirit to you;
I will make my words known to you.
24Because I have called and you refused to listen,
have stretched out my hand and no one has heeded,
25because you have ignored all my counsel
and would have none of my reproof,
26I also will laugh at your calamity;
I will mock when terror strikes you,
27when terror strikes you like a storm
and your calamity comes like a whirlwind,
when distress and anguish come upon you.
28Then they will call upon me, but I will not answer;
they will seek me diligently but will not find me.
29Because they hated knowledge
and did not choose the fear of the LORD,
30would have none of my counsel
and despised all my reproof,

31 therefore they shall eat the fruit of their way,
and have their fill of their own devices.
32 For the simple are killed by their turning away,
and the complacency of fools destroys them;
33 but whoever listens to me will dwell secure
and will be at ease, without dread of disaster.'

'I have called and you refused'

The book of Proverbs has been given to make the people of God wise. It aims to give us insight and understanding so that we know how to deal practically with that messy business of leading our daily lives. I find living quite difficult, especially because I want to do it well. In order to live well, we need wisdom.

So far Proverbs has given us two main topics to think about. The first is the foundation of all knowing, of true knowledge, which comes down to knowing our place before God. The fear of the Lord is the beginning of knowledge (1:7). The second topic was all about going astray, of being seduced into a set of ambitions that is not helpful, that is not based on the fear of the Lord. And we have seen how easily we can be seduced into replacing godly desires with a frame of reference that makes us want to become people who have left living faith behind us.

The final part of chapter 1 forms the next coherent section, which is cast in the form of wisdom speaking directly, as if it were a person, a woman. Wisdom cries out in the street (1:20) and can be heard at the busiest places in town, which are accessible to everyone (1:21). What follows is a direct address from wisdom herself, not a parent instructing their child or words that sinners might use in their seduction, but wisdom speaking directly and publicly. Wisdom is not hidden.

What wisdom is saying here is less encouraging: you simple ones, why are you still not listening to my voice (1:22a)? And turning from the second to the third person, she says that scoffers or cynics love their cynicism and that fools hate knowledge (1:22b). And, because they reject her teaching (1:24–25), she will mock them when the crisis comes, that moment in life when you need loads of experience and real wisdom (1:26). Then she will not be there: wisdom will no longer be available (1:28). And the fools, the scoffers and the simple have only themselves to blame since they rejected wisdom when they could have heeded her instruction (1:29–30). But, once they pass that point of no return, they will eat the fruit of their own ways (1:31), which is of course a beautiful example of mixing the metaphors of travel and fruticulture.

What I find striking from a New Testament perspective is how similar the description of listening to wisdom is to that of the preaching of the gospel. Both offer to make wise and to teach by pouring out the spirit (1:23). Take for example the parable of the ten virgins – five were foolish and five were wise – in Matthew 25:1–13: at a point in this parable, it became too late for the foolish virgins to go into the feast with the wise ones. The pattern is close to what we have here in Proverbs 1. Moreover, Jesus says about himself, 'You will seek me and you will not find me' (John 7:34), just as at some point it will have become too late to learn wisdom (Proverbs 1:28), using very similar words. Hence Paul says that Christ has become our wisdom, from which the term 'wisdom Christology' was coined.

But how are we to understand this passage today, without a specific focus on Jesus Christ? Most obviously, wisdom tells us that it is dangerous, even potentially lethal, to ignore the pursuit of wisdom. The time may come when there is no longer an opportunity or space to acquire it, when you need that wise mind more than ever.

Many of us see our studies for master's or doctoral degrees as a distinct, disconnected part of the rest of our lives – a hoop we have to jump through so that we can start our real mission. It may take a number of years, but it is still nothing more than a temporary inconvenience. Lady Wisdom is telling you to take note. Because today, and tomorrow and the rest of the week, you are determining the person you are going to be. You cannot ignore wisdom now and fool yourself by saying that you will lead a godly and wise life once you have secured a teaching position or a post-doc, or whatever comes next.

Practically this comes down to, for example, your life as part of a local church, a church where there is accountability, where there are people who are not the same as you, where you, bright mind that you are, still sit under the word of God spoken by others, and where you serve. You cannot ignore the wisdom that is taught in Scripture in that we are part of a local body of believers, including everything that comes with it. And, to be honest, a college chapel, a fellowship group or any parachurch gathering won't do it. They are good things but they are not church. You cannot freewheel your way through the years of your PhD. Do not postpone becoming the person you know you should be. Do not think that different rules apply when you are doing your doctorate. Listen to wisdom now and lead a life in the fear of the Lord.

Two key words in our passage add something to the picture that is being painted. The first is that of 'reproof', or rebuke or correction, as found in verses 23, 25 and 30. Accepting wisdom is not just about being shown the direction in which we should travel. At times, it is also about being told that we are doing things wrong. A rebuke can be hard to accept. Yet correction can be not only hard to accept but hard even to hear.

One of the most telling examples I have seen was a student who had worked on a chapter, which they took to their supervisor, who responded by saying that he was not convinced yet and that the argument needed more work. The student worked on it for six weeks and took it back to the supervisor. The response was similar. Several weeks later the same scenario played out for the third time. The now desperate student cried out, 'Do you want me to drop the whole thing then?' To which the supervisor answered, 'That is what I have been telling you the whole time!'

Was this miscommunication a cultural thing? Perhaps. Was it the inability of the student to hear criticism? Quite likely. But, whatever it was, it resulted in a less than productive three months. An anecdote in a devotional book is rarely what postgraduate students dream of as their lasting contribution.

Seeking wisdom includes seeking rebuke and correction. As followers of Christ in the academy, we need that correction because there are so many ways in which the voice of wisdom and faithful perseverance can be dimmed by our own thickheadedness: '"How long, O simple ones, will you love being simple?"' (1:22).

The second key word is the Hebrew word for 'terror' or 'dread', which is found three times in verses 26, 27 and 33.

Terror is a fruit that grows when we reject wisdom. Whereas wisdom grounds us in common sense, in stepping forward carefully, in listening to wisdom's direction and correction, terror appears when we have lost our bearings and are confronted with the insufficiency of our own devices. We are lost, tossed about by whatever fear presents itself and without any plan or understanding. In this passage terror is the result of rejecting wisdom.

Many of the fears we face have to do with a lack of wisdom. A lack of wisdom is a factor in the permanent panic that we are supposed to feel when reading the news. Yet we can turn this around. We could use our own unwise fears to identify areas in our life where we need to grow in wisdom. And the good thing is that we are here to help one another.

Wisdom speaks now, openly and publicly. Do not ignore the call to become wise. Think and reflect and learn. You may need to accept correction, that you have been doing things the wrong way. That is fine. Change hurts less than continuing on the wrong path. And your terror can be the result of an absence of wisdom. Take note, do not be complacent but start again from the basis, from the fear of the Lord that is the beginning of all knowledge and wisdom.

For further reflection

1 How do we solve the tension between wisdom being so widely available but also hard to acquire in practice?
2 How do we keep on encouraging one another to pursue wisdom?
3 How does wisdom relate to the gospel? How do they differ and how are they similar?

Knowing good and evil

Romans 16:17–20

[17]I appeal to you, brothers, to watch out for those who cause divisions and create obstacles contrary to the doctrine that you have been taught; avoid them. [18]For such persons do not serve our Lord Christ, but their own appetites, and by smooth talk and flattery they deceive the hearts of the naive. [19]For your obedience is known to all, so that I rejoice over you, but I want you to be wise as to what is good and innocent as to what is evil. [20]The God of peace will soon crush Satan under your feet. The grace of our Lord Jesus Christ be with you.

'Innocent as to what is evil'

Romans 16 contains the highest concentration of personal names in the New Testament outside the genealogies of the Gospels. Though Paul has not visited Rome at the time of writing, he takes time to point out the many personal relationships he already has with various people in the church there. This list comes to an end in 16:16, where Paul moves to conveying greetings from others – 'All the churches of Christ greet you' – and likewise in 16:21, 'Timothy, my fellow worker, greets you; so do Lucius and Jason and Sosipater.' But what about the little section tucked in between, Romans 16:17–20, which is, according to 16:17, an 'appeal'? What is it doing in the middle of all these greetings from Paul and others?

We can do little more than try to second-guess Paul, but it is worth asking the question. Might this appeal be a mere afterthought, something dropped in as a little encore? That is unlikely. It usually pays to give Scripture more credit than to regard a detail as just a random addition without a wider function.

What then? Might it be that after such a long list of people who are greeted by name, there are also some notable absences? And could these be people who have deliberately not been greeted because they need to be warned against? We do not know, but a scenario such as this could explain the curious position of this little section.

Paul urges the church 'to watch out for those who cause divisions' (16:17), who are further specified as those who put obstacles in the way contrary to the received doctrine. In this particular instance the advice is simple: avoid them!

The divisions and obstacles created by them may well be the divisions mentioned in the previous chapters of Romans, but at the same time this passage is sufficiently far removed from those earlier discussions to suggest that the focus is much wider than specific Roman issues. If so, Paul's appeal becomes even easier to apply to our own situations.

How are these troublemakers described? Without mincing his words, Paul says that they 'do not serve our Lord Christ, but their own appetites' (Greek *koilia*, 'belly'). In Philippians 3:19, Paul tells us that for some wicked people their belly is their god. Being self-serving lies at the heart of much false teaching and attempts to lure people away from the gospel. And the reason why so often these wolves are not recognised for what they are is because of 'their smooth talk and flattery' (16:18). They deceive naive people with the weapons of smooth words, and experience teaches that a surprising number of us turn out to be more naive than we would have expected. It is Genesis 3 and the garden of Eden all over again.

The church of Rome is at risk, 'for your obedience is known to all' (16:19). As wasps are attracted to sweet lemonade at the end of summer, so an obedient church attracts deceivers. But Paul remains positive. Apart from avoiding them in the first place, the only real protection against these people and their talk is simply to continue obeying the taught doctrine – but not naively. Paul desires us to be wise in what is good but innocent in evil. This still means avoiding those who cause divisions and obeying the doctrine as received, but as warned people. And Paul slips in a second reference to Genesis 3 and the garden of Eden in bringing good and evil together. There is no need to eat of the fruit and to know good and to know evil, even though it is 'to be desired to make one wise' (Genesis 3:6). It is much healthier to be wise in what is good and innocent in what is evil.

In 16:20 we learn that wisdom sees beyond the person. The church may have thought that they were dealing with people who were simply in need of a proper explanation of the truth, but this is not Paul's assessment. The one who will be crushed under our feet is Satan himself (Genesis 3:15), as the ultimate deceiver, full of flattery and smooth talk. The fight is not against flesh and blood but, in the context of the spiritual battle, Satan himself, whom Paul identifies as behind all this.

It is worthwhile thinking a little more about the phrase 'wise as to what is good and innocent as to what is evil' in

Romans 16:19. Recall the story of the two trees in the garden of Eden: 'The tree of life was in the midst of the garden, and the tree of the knowledge of good and evil' (Genesis 2:9). Then God gives an – at first sight – rather curious commandment regarding one of the trees, 'You may surely eat of every tree of the garden, but of the tree of the knowledge of good and evil you shall not eat, for in the day that you eat of it you shall surely die' (Genesis 2:16–17). Why is the newly created human race not allowed to do something that seems so perfectly reasonable? What is wrong with knowing good and evil? Isn't a basic requirement of living your life before God to know what is evil? The serpent plays on this and describes some of the consequences of eating – and does so correctly: 'For God knows that when you eat of it your eyes will be opened, and you will be like God, knowing good and evil' (Genesis 3:5). God himself confirms this a little later, 'Behold, the man has become like one of us in knowing good and evil' (Genesis 3:22).

So what is wrong with knowing good and evil? How can you do the right thing otherwise? Why is it okay for God but lethal for humans to know good and evil? The first part of the answer is that Genesis itself explains very quickly that 'knowing' is much more than knowing something about something. Knowing in the biblical sense means having a close relationship with something. Take, for example, Genesis 4:1, which the New International Version (NIV) translates as 'Adam made love to his wife Eve' but which many translations, retaining the Hebrew wording, translate as 'Adam knew his wife Eve'. Clearly, 'knowing' is something intimate; it is relational. Knowledge is also not neutral, for it does something to us. You cannot unsee things – it changes us. So what happens when created and weak human beings know evil? We get polluted by the evil we know. We cannot resist its effects. We do not overcome the evil we know but evil overcomes us. Knowing evil does something to us, and what it does is not good. Unlike God, we are simply not strong enough. We are weak and have been made to live in dependence on the life of our Father.

To illustrate this, what happens when someone carries food that is ritually clean and touches something that is unclean (Haggai 2:11–13)? For us humans, holiness is not transferred to something unclean but instead the unclean thing makes the holy food unclean. Then there is Jesus. It is remarkable how often the Gospels tell us that he touched a sick person or a sick person touched Jesus and was healed. The holiness and the life of Jesus were stronger than the sin and impurity of the human beings around him. They became clean because the good of God is stronger than any evil. That is the difference between the weak human and the eternal God: he overcomes evil, while we are weak and succumb to the knowledge of evil.

And that is why the tree of the knowledge of good and evil is not good for us. It illustrates the difference between God and us. We are made to be dependent on the life that God gives because we are not strong enough to survive knowing evil. This text shows a better way to relate to good and evil: 'be wise as to what is good and innocent as to what is evil' (Romans 16:19).

We started by speculating about the positioning of these verses among all those greeted and greeting people. All of them have names. But so do the deceivers, even though their names are not mentioned. These deceivers are real people.

Perhaps they do their smooth talking in your churches, or you meet them at conferences or in your departments. These may well be people you know personally. You may get on with them. They may be people who confide in you, who have their joys, their struggles. You may spend an evening in the pub with them, have a laugh and keep as your Facebook friends. These are people with names, who sometimes best remain unnamed. When Paul says that it is best to avoid certain people, he knows that he is talking about real human beings with names.

There may be certain people whom you and I know whom we should avoid because of what they do to the church, because they are serving their own belly, because of their smooth talk and our own naivety, because we need to be innocent as to what is evil and because Satan will be crushed by him who is here described as the God of peace.

I pray that each of us will be wise as to what is good, in distinguishing between those who need to be drawn out of the fire and those whom we'd better avoid.

For further reflection

1. Have you ever experienced or come across cases where smooth talk and flattery are used as an obstacle against the teaching of the gospel?
2. How would you respond to someone who says to you, 'I think I am strong enough as a Christian to cope with this dangerous knowledge'?
3. How does the saying 'The fear of the Lord is the beginning of knowledge' (Proverbs 1:7) relate to being 'wise as to what is good and innocent as to what is evil'? (See the chapter 'To become wise I: Where to begin?)

Listening to God

Hebrews 1:1 – 2:1

1:1 Long ago, at many times and in many ways, God spoke
to our fathers by the prophets, 2 but in these last days he
has spoken to us by his Son, whom he appointed the heir
of all things, through whom also he created the world. 3 He
is the radiance of the glory of God and the exact imprint of
his nature, and he upholds the universe by the word of his
power. After making purification for sins, he sat down at the
right hand of the Majesty on high, 4 having become as much
superior to angels as the name he has inherited is more
excellent than theirs.

5 For to which of the angels did God ever say,
'You are my Son,
today I have begotten you'?
Or again,
'I will be to him a father,
and he shall be to me a son'?
6 And again, when he brings the firstborn into the world, he
says,
'Let all God's angels worship him.'
7 Of the angels he says,
'He makes his angels winds,
and his ministers a flame of fire.'
8 But of the Son he says,
'Your throne, O God, is for ever and ever,

the sceptre of uprightness is the sceptre of your
kingdom.
9You have loved righteousness and hated wickedness;
therefore God, your God, has anointed you
with the oil of gladness beyond your companions.'
10And,
'You, Lord, laid the foundation of the earth in the
beginning,
and the heavens are the work of your hands;
11they will perish, but you remain;
they will all wear out like a garment,
12like a robe you will roll them up,
like a garment they will be changed.
But you are the same,
and your years will have no end.'
13And to which of the angels has he ever said,
'Sit at my right hand
until I make your enemies a footstool for your feet'?
14Are they not all ministering spirits sent out to serve for
the sake of those who are to inherit salvation?
2:1Therefore we must pay much closer attention to what we
have heard, lest we drift away from it.

God speaks

The Christian social culture has some peculiar quirks. One of these is that there seems to exist a particular category of people or, perhaps better, a class of people, who can style themselves as 'speaker'. The label 'speaker', apparently, indicates membership of a pool of individuals who are invited to deliver talks at Christian meetings and conferences. 'Who are you?' 'I am a speaker!' You can almost hear the capital S at the beginning of the word. Of course, not a few of those who put 'speaker' in their social media profile have an ambition to receive all the prestigious invitations and are simply advertising their availability.

To be a speaker is quite a desirable status in many fields, not just in Christianity. Yet the position does not come with a quality guarantee. You may have sat through many a talk or lecture thinking that you would have done a much better job (I certainly have). The thought of addressing a crowd is good for our self-esteem: we like having people look up to us.

We are all taught by contemporary culture that the ambition to become famous is a good thing – and also that pride is not a deadly sin. To be a speaker, you need stage presence, a good turn of phrase, access to a big library of emotion-stirring personal stories and to have written a book or two. Expertise in anything is entirely optional.

One reason for this caricature is to illustrate the power of the spoken word. Speech impresses itself on us in ways that writing does not. And this distinction is found in Scripture. John writes in his second letter that he has much to write but 'would rather not use paper and ink. Instead I hope to come to you and talk face to face, so that our joy may be complete' (2 John 12).

Now all this leads to a pressing question. Are we as Christians, as students of Holy Scripture, at a disadvantage in having to deal with the written word rather than with God talking to us directly? Is the Bible, which is rightly called the word of God, a second-best option, something we have to put up with in the absence of a more direct self-revelation of our God?

If we start with the Bible's self-designation, we find many references to its own written character. 'Scripture' and 'Scriptures' are frequently used terms. Moses wrote (Exodus 24:4), as did Isaiah (2 Chronicles 26:22). Quite a few of the biblical authors refer to their own writing activity or were explicitly instructed to write their words down. The Bible is a written book, and we are encouraged to think of it as such.

Academic studies also encourage us to think of the Bible as a book. The Bible is compared with other documents from the ancient Near East. Scholars trawl through the writings from Qumran and other contemporary literature to learn more about the background of the New Testament. We debate the genre of the Gospels on the basis of a comparison with Greek and Roman authors. We apply literary criticism in all its forms. We treat the Bible as a book that is written, copied and translated. All this is true and good, and some of it is even helpful. But at the same time it is an incomplete story. And that is where Hebrews helps us to grow further in our understanding of what Scripture is.

Hebrews starts off reminding us that God spoke by prophets in former days but now, in these last days, by his Son. This is then followed by the briefest description of the nature of Christ in verses 2–4 and, jumping straight to 2:1, we find that we have heard this message. The remainder of chapter 1 is a pastiche of seven Old Testament citations. How are these citations introduced? There are three places where we have a verb introducing the citation: 'God … say' (1:5); 'he says' (1:6); 'he says' (1:7).

If we were to continue this exercise throughout the letter to the Hebrews we will not find a single instance where a citation of the Old Testament is introduced with 'as it is written' or words with a similar meaning; it is always a verb of speaking. The Old Testament fills much of the letter to the Hebrews not so much as 'Scripture' but rather as a spoken word. We read that God spoke in or through David (4:7). Other parts of this letter use words to the effect that God says, or Christ says, or the Holy Spirit says to introduce citations of written Scripture. In the same way the whole letter reads like spoken language (e.g., Hebrews 5:11; 8:1; 11:32). It is only in 13:22 that the written nature of this document is referred to ('I have written to you briefly'); before this it could have been a spoken sermon. It is remarkable how the letter to the Hebrews refers to the Bible as the spoken word of God, which God *has spoken* and *is speaking*, even though it is not blind to the mediated way in which God's word came to believers. God is the one who speaks the Psalms; he is the one who speaks the Prophets.

This view of Scripture sets it apart from any other type of writing. God is presented as still speaking in Scripture with an immediacy that cannot be claimed for any other work. What we read in Scripture are words that have been written down, which need to be translated, weighed, pursued, compared and carefully studied. But if the Bible were to remain a historical object, we miss out on what Scripture testifies about itself. Contrary to our distinction between speaking and writing, in the divine communication we read the written word and we hear not just what God said but also what he *is saying*.

Of course, we use the language of printed words that speak of all sorts of writing, not just the Bible. Poets speak from beyond the grave. In court we ask what the law says. And these expressions reinforce the point. Yet, in Scripture we have a further claim: that it is the word of someone who lives. It is the word of a speaker who is present.

How does this affect our work as readers of God's revelation? There are a number of different ways we can respond. One is to take note of the phenomenon, explain it as something that is peculiar to the author of Hebrews and store it in our collection of historical curiosities in Scripture. Another option is to read ourselves into the story and to take seriously the warning, 'Today, if you hear his voice …' as Christians who read what God has said and what he is saying in Scripture, and realise that we are committed to hearing his voice.

Our subject matter is not a distant word written on tablets or parchment. Rather, it is the voice of the living God, who is speaking with authority and a richness that has defied thousands of PhDs and is not hindered by any medium or human mediator. God speaks and he tells us about the Son, who purified us, who opened our ears so that we have ears to hear and who implants his word in us so that we are made ready to live for him: 'Therefore we must pay much closer attention to what we have heard' (2:1). Irrespective of our academic specialisation, and in the context of the thousands of words we read throughout the week, as Christians who have heard and met the word of life, we reserve a special status for the word that has given us life.

For further reflection

1 There are a number of different ways to read the Bible: as history, as literature, as accounts of religious experience and so on. How does Hebrews 1 and its

introduction to citations from the Old Testament encourage us to read?

2 How does Scripture draw you closer to God?
3 What are some of the practical obstacles that hinder you from fully engaging with God's word? Try to examine these obstacles a little more.

Common sense

Hebrews 13:1–25

[1]Let brotherly love continue. [2]Do not neglect to show hospitality to strangers, for thereby some have entertained angels unawares. [3]Remember those who are in prison, as though in prison with them, and those who are mistreated, since you also are in the body. [4]Let marriage be held in honour among all, and let the marriage bed be undefiled, for God will judge the sexually immoral and adulterous. [5]Keep your life free from love of money, and be content with what you have, for he has said, 'I will never leave you nor forsake you.' [6]So we can confidently say,

'The Lord is my helper;
  I will not fear;
what can man do to me?'

[7]Remember your leaders, those who spoke to you the word of God. Consider the outcome of their way of life, and imitate their faith. [8]Jesus Christ is the same yesterday and today and for ever. [9]Do not be led away by diverse and strange teachings, for it is good for the heart to be strengthened by grace, not by foods, which have not benefited those devoted to them. [10]We have an altar from which those who serve the tent have no right to eat. [11]For the bodies of those animals whose blood is brought into the holy places by the high priest as a sacrifice for sin are burned outside the camp. [12]So Jesus also suffered outside the gate in order to sanctify the people through his own blood. [13]Therefore let us go to him outside the camp and bear the reproach he

endured. [14]For here we have no lasting city, but we seek the
city that is to come. [15]Through him then let us continually
offer up a sacrifice of praise to God, that is, the fruit of lips
that acknowledge his name. [16]Do not neglect to do good
and to share what you have, for such sacrifices are pleasing
to God.

[17]Obey your leaders and submit to them, for they are
keeping watch over your souls, as those who will have to give
an account. Let them do this with joy and not with groaning,
for that would be of no advantage to you.

[18]Pray for us, for we are sure that we have a clear con-
science, desiring to act honourably in all things. [19]I urge you
the more earnestly to do this in order that I may be restored
to you the sooner.

[20]Now may the God of peace who brought again from the
dead our Lord Jesus, the great shepherd of the sheep, by the
blood of the eternal covenant, [21]equip you with everything
good that you may do his will, working in us that which is
pleasing in his sight, through Jesus Christ, to whom be glory
for ever and ever. Amen.

[22]I appeal to you, brothers, bear with my word of exhort-
ation, for I have written to you briefly. [23]You should know
that our brother Timothy has been released, with whom I
shall see you if he comes soon. [24]Greet all your leaders and
all the saints. Those who come from Italy send you greetings.
[25]Grace be with all of you.

'For it is good'

One of the things I have learned from being in Cambridge is that intelligence and a good education do not help people to know how to live better. Life is no less of a struggle for the well trained than it is for those with fewer formal qualifications. And, according to quite a few people – among them my wife, a professional counsellor – and in line with the caricature, the typical academic may be less adapted to the simple challenges of normal life.

What might be the reason behind this? Apart from a more general clumsiness or an obsession with the cerebral over the relational and the practical, one reason may well be that we, as educated people, think that everything needs to be done by specialists. We expect special knowledge to be required for any challenging task, whether it be changing a light bulb, adjusting the thermostat in our room, getting rid of weeds in our garden or repairing a bike. We assume that specialist knowledge is required because we ourselves are striving to become specialists and to make ourselves equally indispensable. Let me gently prick your bubble. For most of life the only thing you need is not a formal degree or an educational qualification, but simple old-fashioned common sense.

But what about the transformed Christian life? How does the new life in Christ make a difference over and above common sense? Is Christian wisdom more than just a restored sense of what is right and just and fitting?

Hebrews 13 is a fascinating chapter that helps us to look at these questions. This passage comes on the back of twelve chapters of exegetical and theological fireworks urging the readers to put their wholehearted trust in Jesus as the supreme, eternal high priest. He can save completely, he can reconcile completely and he instructs completely. We are to pay close attention to what is spoken by God both in the Scriptures of the old covenant and the proclamation of the new. The reader has been instructed about the right direction of their heart and urged to focus on the heavenly and exalted Christ and the reality of the world that is to come.

And then the final chapter of this book brings that whole narrative world of a heavenly temple and Christ seated at the right hand of God to bear on our daily lives – not by giving a forced application but by showing how this complex of scriptural images and Old Testament narrative becomes our new common sense. Hebrews 13 shows how Scripture is lived out, how the patterns and categories that drive salvation history play out in normal life.

In this chapter we have thirteen imperatives and two pairs of verbless clauses that work like commands.[1] And then there are two exhortations in the first-person plural 'let us' (verses 13 and 15). Most of these seventeen commands have an explanation attached: do this for such and such a reason.[2] These reasons largely resonate with the patterns found in Scripture and are easily traceable. The word of God becomes our common sense.

In verse 1 the first command is for something to continue, 'Let brotherly love [Greek *philadelphia*] continue.' In chapter 6, the author had praised his readers for their service to the saints: let that attitude simply continue. Scholars and scientists tend to do reasonably well in this regard. I have seen people guarding their ideas quite anxiously, or at very rare occasions even copying them from others without source acknowledgement, but on average there is a certain camaraderie (until the point where research groups compete

1 Verses 4 and 5 do not have a verb in the original Greek: 'let … be held', 'let … be', 'keep' and 'be' have all been added in the English translation since English sentences demand a verb.

2 There is a 'for' in Hebrews 13:2, 4, 5, 9, 14, 16, 17, 18 and 22.

for money or prestige). Yet, when asked to what extent this sibling love reaches non-scholars as well, quite a few academics are bored and have to work hard to show a genuine interest in others.

Verse 2 moves from sibling love (*philadelphia*) to visitor love (*philoxenia*). This is the first command in this chapter with an attached 'for' clause. Hospitality is a good thing, as people in the Old Testament were hosting angels without realising it initially, normally with positive consequences. Think of Lot, for example, who saved his life by opening his house up. Hospitality is good and sometimes for totally unexpected reasons, which is why academics are good at it. Admittedly, hospitality is not always selfless. We may be thinking about building a network that could be helpful for jobs or other opportunities. There is nothing wrong with this, as long as hospitality is real hospitality and not just shameless cosying up to the rich and powerful while ignoring the poor and powerless. Real hospitality will be rewarded, if not now then certainly later.

The next command does not have an explanation in the form of a 'for' such and such a reason. Remember those in prison and remember those who are mistreated (the Greek verb means something like 'to have it bad'). The first group ought to be remembered as if we were their fellow prisoners, and those who are mistreated as we also are in a body that can suffer the same abuse. The whole notion of suffering with one's brothers and sisters is pervasive throughout the Law. It is a healthy antidote to individualism and the myth of the self-made man. Within the guild of scholarship we can easily relate to the struggles and sufferings of our colleagues, but the intended audience of Hebrews is not determined by job or occupation. The audience is the whole people of God: all those who belong to Jesus, not just those who have higher degrees.

Next, 'Let marriage be held in honour among all' (13:4). This is directed at both those who are married and those who are not, as is the following command: 'let the marriage bed be undefiled'. It is a little puzzling why the translators have added 'marriage' here. After all, sexual purity is a matter as much for those who are married as it is for those who are not married. Again we have an explanation, for 'God will judge the sexually immoral and adulterous'. The Old Testament shows throughout how God hates sexual immorality.[3] Statistics for the consumption of pornography are horrendous, including among Christians. Take all sin in your life seriously, especially sexual impurity. For God will judge the sexually immoral and adulterous.

The following imperatives work similarly. In 13:5 the reason for not loving money is 'for he has said …'. In 13:9 the reference to true food for the heart is presented as a better alternative than studying obscure or strange teachings. In 13:16 generosity is encouraged, for that is the type of sacrifice God loves. In 13:17 the accountability of leaders to God is given as a reason for the reader to trust and submit to them. Again, look at Moses or David to see what such accountability means.

We could go on, but the sum of it all is that Hebrews calls us not only to understand Scripture, to understand all of it

---

3 Leviticus 18 lists a variety of illegitimate sexual relations, adding the warning that 'by all these the nations I am driving out before you have become unclean, and the land became unclean, so that I punished its iniquity, and the land vomited out its inhabitants' (18:24–25). Adultery is one of the main metaphors in the Bible to describe what it means to abandon God and cling to other things to worship (e.g. Hosea 2).

in its telling of the great plan of God's salvation, but also to live Scripture: to copy its wisdom and its sound patterns of behaviour; to sit at its feet to be instructed in how to live, act and respond; to feed our hearts and souls with its true food and true guidance. Scripture then becomes our new common sense. There is no such thing as overexposure to Scripture. It teaches wisdom to the clumsy.

For further reflection

1 What is the relation between Christian wisdom and common sense?
2 Looking at the first three reasons for living well in 13:1, 4 and 5–6, what makes the result specifically Christian? Or is only the motivation Christian and not the result?
3 How important is it for the argument in Hebrews 13 that the reader knows Scripture well?

Words and power

Galatians 1:6–9

[6]I am astonished that you are so quickly deserting him who called you in the grace of Christ and are turning to a different gospel – [7]not that there is another one, but there are some who trouble you and want to distort the gospel of Christ. [8]But even if we or an angel from heaven should preach to you a gospel contrary to the one we preached to you, let him be accursed. [9]As we have said before, so now I say again: If anyone is preaching to you a gospel contrary to the one you received, let him be accursed.

Let him be accursed

Not every part of the Bible has the same internal pace: stories and arguments can develop slowly or quickly. Some stories, such as the story of David and Absalom, which takes up several chapters, are told at a slow pace. Likewise the dialogue between Job and his friends is slow; the poetic imagery is rich but each turn in the conversation takes many words. Other parts of the Bible are the opposite and have been written in dense language. The letters to the Galatians and Ephesians are good examples, which together take up less space than the narrative about David and Absalom. Likewise, in the Sermon on the Mount every sentence demands extensive unpacking.

This is only one way to study the language of Scripture. A different way has gained traction in recent decades, inspired by deconstructionist theories, where we are encouraged to find the hidden agenda behind any piece of writing.[1] Here, we might ask how the letter to the Galatians functions as a power dynamic and what Paul is really trying to achieve through it. In such an approach we might point out that Paul conflates the word of God with his own preaching. He claims divine authority for himself, all as part of an agenda to sideline his rivals. Ultimately, Paul's main goal is to confirm his position of power over the churches.

This is not the most sympathetic way of reading Paul, and it assumes that his motives are not what he claims. It is more productive, I think, to take Paul at his word and to read Galatians as inspired Scripture. Paul's gospel is God's gospel, and deserting the gospel that Paul preaches is deserting God himself who has called us. As Jude writes, there is 'the faith that was once for all delivered to the saints' (Jude 3). And John also tells us that he is not writing a new commandment but only what his readers had heard 'from the beginning' (1 John 2:7). There is a completeness and finality in the revelation that God has given us in the writings of the New Testament through his apostles.

Of course, this finality raises all sorts of questions for us as thoughtful readers of Scripture. Where do we draw the line between innovation and conservation? Is the only thing left to us to repeat again and again the things that have already been said? Is it not built into the DNA of the academy to produce new knowledge? When is originality no longer a virtue? Clearly, some so-called original ideas are original

1 I want to draw a stark line between Scripture as God's word to us and any other discourse. Scripture's goal is to bring us close to God not by deceit or by duplicity; it is pure. Any human communication is, to a certain degree, polluted by personal and cultural motives and therefore contains material that lends itself to critical analysis. Still, keep in mind that modern authors may also have good intentions.

only because they are so clearly wrong. We may have seen desperate attempts by young scholars to say something new, to be distinctive and ultimately to get a name and a following for themselves. Academics can act a little bit like the Athenians in Acts 17:21 who 'spend their time in nothing except telling or hearing something new'. And, though many strive to say something new and many claim to do so, it is remarkable how few actually succeed. There are many misguided claims to originality.

Still, it is too easy to be cynical about scholarship. There is a genuine place for developing new knowledge, even within the 'soft' arts and humanities and this also includes further study of God's revelation. Even though we may start from the notion that the gospel is a once-for-all event, perfect and complete in how it happened and how it has been revealed to us, we still have to acknowledge that its implications and effects are so magnificent that there is space for an endless stream of doctoral projects, books and personal studies. If we say that there is nothing left to study, we show that we have a rather small view of the gospel and of everything that God has done in this world.

The argument of this passage is not particularly complicated. Paul was appointed by God the Father and Jesus Christ, and had a gospel to share that tells of what the Father and the Son have done for our salvation. This was what Paul received and what he has preached. However, his readers have apparently been exposed to some 'who trouble' them (1:7), who distort the gospel of Christ and lead people to desert 'him who called [them] in the grace of Christ' (1:6).

For Paul the uniqueness and the completeness of the revealed gospel meant that he had a robust starting point from which to address the current troubles in the churches of Galatia. But at the same time, with ruthless honesty, he talks about one of the consequences of this completeness. It means something for his own subsequent gospel ministry: 'even if we or an angel from heaven should preach to you a gospel contrary to the one we preached to you, let him be accursed' (1:8). And for good measure he repeats this in the next verse.

Is this just hyperbole? Is Paul exaggerating for rhetorical effect? Again, we could deconstruct these words and say rather smugly that Paul is such a clever player of the power game in using these words to establish his own authoritative position. But what if we were to take these strong words as they stand, if we were to see these as people who know that God is speaking in Scripture? The fierceness of Paul's words is clearly meant to emphasise what is at stake: 'If anyone is preaching to you a gospel contrary to the one you received, let him be accursed' (verse 9). For Paul, the preaching of the gospel was so important that any distortion of the message warrants calling for a curse.

In the New Testament there is not a big difference between teaching and preaching the gospel.[2] Many of us who are active in higher education get opportunities to teach and lead in our churches. After all, we are trained to explain stuff to others. Paul does not hesitate to say that if he were to preach a gospel against what he had preached before, he should be accursed. This is how aware he is of how, like Moses at the burning bush, he is standing on holy ground when preaching the gospel.

---

2 See, for example, Luke 20:1: 'One day, as Jesus was teaching the people in the temple and preaching the gospel …'.

Every so often I realise with horror how careless I am with my words, how easy it is to say bold things I shouldn't say, how easy it is to pontificate about things I do not fully understand. Being a New Testament scholar can fill me with dread. Compare that with Paul's grave reflection on explaining the gospel: 'even if we … should preach to you a gospel contrary to the one we preached to you, let him be accursed.'

What about those of us who have a permanent teaching office: have we thought through how our teaching relates to the gospel? Do I dare to say anything knowing that studying and teaching and preaching the gospel has such high stakes? If I teach in this book a gospel against what has been once for all delivered to the church, let me be accursed. Do we realise what is at stake? What about when we prepare and lead a Bible study in church or for a fellowship group: would I dare to put this verse on the wall when I am working on a study?

As a teacher I stumble in many ways (James 3:1–2), but this is not the end. Often I don't reflect the gospel in its generosity, its patience and its love and grace. Rather than being slow to speak, I am too quick to get my words in. I am not competent in the role of a teacher. But just as Paul was called to be an apostle not by man but by God, so is our competency not from ourselves but from him who called us to our roles. And I thank God that he called us not under the law and the fear of breaking rules but, as Galatians 1:6 says, he 'called [us] in the grace of Christ'. The grace by which we have been called is not just the grace that lies at the heart of the gospel message but it is also the grace I need to carry out my studies. It is the grace that is so powerful, so important and so glorious that it can take our feeble and imperfect efforts and transform them into tools for the gospel. It is the grace I need to carry on doing my work. It is the grace I need to properly think through the gospel of grace.

For further reflection

1 What are the differences between how we study and teach in the academy and how we preach the gospel?
2 What are the parts of the gospel message that, if we get them wrong, fall into the 'let me be accursed' category?
3 What is the role of grace in our teaching of the gospel?

Persuasion

Galatians 4:12–20

12Brothers, I entreat you, become as I am, for I also have
become as you are. You did me no wrong. 13You know it was
because of a bodily ailment that I preached the gospel to you
at first, 14and though my condition was a trial to you, you
did not scorn or despise me, but received me as an angel of
God, as Christ Jesus. 15What then has become of the blessing
you felt? For I testify to you that, if possible, you would have
gouged out your eyes and given them to me. 16Have I then
become your enemy by telling you the truth? 17They make
much of you, but for no good purpose. They want to shut
you out, that you may make much of them. 18It is always
good to be made much of for a good purpose, and not only
when I am present with you, 19my little children, for whom I
am again in the anguish of childbirth until Christ is formed
in you! 20I wish I could be present with you now and change
my tone, for I am perplexed about you.

'I am … in the anguish of childbirth'

In a previous chapter ('To become wise II: Seduction') we thought about the process by which someone's values can be changed so dramatically that they end up with the wrong crowd. People are seduced by the promise of a seat at the table and the respect of those to whom they look up. In Proverbs the warning was cast in the form of a father and mother's warning to their son. The situation in Galatians 4 is somewhat similar.

Paul sees the churches in Galatia slipping away because people are working to wean the believers off the gospel as preached by the apostles. Most of the letter addresses their arguments, but Paul also devotes space to the human aspect: 'Remember the good times we had together. Remember what we had together. How could you forget the fellowship we had?'

So far there have been a number of harsh expressions in the letter: 'I am astonished that you are so quickly deserting him who called you' (1:6); 'O foolish Galatians' (3:1); 'Are you so foolish? ... Did you suffer so many things in vain ...?' (3:3–4). Likewise, the words immediately preceding our passage are not particularly gentle: 'how can you turn back again?' (4:9); 'I am afraid I may have laboured over you in vain' (4:11). Paul is not creating a safe space in his letters where people can feel at home and be simply affirmed in all that they are; on the contrary, he does not coddle but confronts them. But he does not confront from a distance or from a position of emotional coldness: rather, he invests his whole self and all his emotional capital in trying to win the Galatians back. He is not putting up a front of male bravado but speaks about suffering labour pains again in giving birth to the Galatian churches, applying exclusively motherly terms to himself.

So how does this work out in what Paul writes? In 4:12 he sets up a comparison or, perhaps better, a balance of mutual appreciation: 'become as I am, for I also have become as you are.' How should the Galatians become like Paul? To paraphrase: 'my attitude towards you is that you have done nothing wrong to me.' And then the thought breaks off. What is implied is, of course, that their attitude towards

Paul ought to be that he has done nothing wrong to them. And this suspended thought, which hangs over the passage, comes to a resolution only in 4:16: 'Have I then become your enemy by telling you the truth?'

Paul is in doubt and perplexed about the Galatians, and he pleads with them to think about him in the same terms as he does about them, neither party having wronged the other. However, not being present, Paul expresses his doubts as to whether they actually feel the same way and wonders if they might even think that Paul is their enemy.

To think of someone as an enemy when they have said some harsh words to you is a very human reaction. As soon as a friend or colleague corrects me, especially when there is something seriously wrong with me, my first instinct is to blame the messenger, to think that they must have something against me. We are perhaps a bit better at separating the message from the messenger when a medic comes with bad news, though even in those circumstances I have seen people analysing every phrase to see whether the doctor is sympathetic. And every emotional misstep is pounced on to reinforce a constructed image of their miserable character. Paul's way of dealing with this dangerous human tendency is not to leave it festering under the surface but to discuss it and to force his readers to confront it.

In between verses 12 and 16, in the space before the thought of 4:12 is finished in 4:16, Paul further undermines the improbable case that he is the unsympathetic messenger with evil intent. In the past the Galatians had appreciated Paul as an angel of God and loved him so much that they would have given their own eyes for him, but now they seem to have lost their sense of having been blessed by Paul.

And Paul, for his part, talks about the pain he is suffering for them, which can be paraphrased as: 'Become like me, in that I think you did me no wrong, because I am like you and am in the anguish of childbirth for you.' Just as the Galatians would have been prepared to gouge out their eyes for Paul (not a particularly pleasant image), so Paul is suffering the pangs of childbirth (not a pleasant experience either, though much more productive).

For readers who are convinced by his plea, Paul opens up a gentle way out of their apparent opposition to the gospel that he preached. In verse 17, the ultimate blame is placed on the agitators in Galatia who are deceiving the churches and enslaving them for their own purpose and to serve themselves. In contrast, Paul is a worried and pained mother.

What is there for us as professional students to learn from this passage? Paul shows that persuasion is not just about arguments but also about addressing the person. So far in this letter we have had narrative history, where the conversion of Paul and his dealings with other apostles who acknowledge him (1:13 – 2:14) have created a context that is very different from the current situation between Paul and the Galatians. We have also had doctrinal argumentation from Scripture (2:15 – 4:7). And then in this passage we have the personal appeal, the sharing of what is at stake on an emotional level, on the level of affections. Persuasion is not just about arguments.

What is needed for effective communication is to establish a willingness to listen to the speaker. And there can be all sort of stumbling blocks that prevent someone from listening. The Galatians appear to have lost much of their previous appreciation of Paul. And Paul is eager to show them how their attitude has changed, that their faded love for him had no cause other than that found in themselves. Paul still has the same commitment.

We are often persuaded not by arguments but by certain prior choices. Sometimes these are sociological: we may have sympathy for a certain group, lifestyle or institution and will be predisposed to accept their argument. Alternatively, we may want to distance ourselves from certain groups and therefore be inclined to reject arguments that sound like they could have been made by them. We may have a poor experience in a church we have long since left, or been hurt by the rigid attitude of parents. Any argument but theirs! We are often already convinced even before listening because of our sympathy with, or aversion towards, a particular social circle or individual.

When we go out to persuade people, we should realise that persuasion is not just about arguments. Of course our thinking must be solid, but we cannot expect to persuade people if we can't give people a reason to want to be persuaded. There is work for us to do. We should always be prepared to give an account of the hope that is in us (1 Peter 3:15).

The academy is supposed to be different, though. In the academy we are supposed to just consider the argument stripped of all human context. There are sometimes situations where this is the case, where it is possible to have these conversations without an underlying agenda, when we can play with ideas or shoot them down, where we can improve the ideas of our opponent and be critical of our own. It does happen but not always.

Most of the time, and especially within the church context, we should realise that we academics are not just functioning as detached providers of clever arguments but are involved as humans with other humans. And this includes our broken histories, our limited understanding and the full force of our emotional commitment and investment in the people we seek to reach and with whom we work. All this so that Christ may be formed in them (4:19).

For further reflection

1. The process of persuasion in the hard sciences is different from in the arts and humanities. How does persuasion happen between Christians? What are some good and poor examples you have experienced?
2. How does this chapter apply to evangelism and sharing your faith with colleagues?
3. How can you pray for more opportunities to share your faith alongside honing your persuasive skill set?

Working with joy

Philippians 1:15–26

[15]Some indeed preach Christ from envy and rivalry, but others from good will. [16]The latter do it out of love, knowing that I am put here for the defence of the gospel. [17]The former proclaim Christ out of selfish ambition, not sincerely but thinking to afflict me in my imprisonment. [18]What then? Only that in every way, whether in pretence or in truth, Christ is proclaimed, and in that I rejoice.

Yes, and I will rejoice, [19]for I know that through your prayers and the help of the Spirit of Jesus Christ this will turn out for my deliverance, [20]as it is my eager expectation and hope that I will not be at all ashamed, but that with full courage now as always Christ will be honoured in my body, whether by life or by death. [21]For to me to live is Christ, and to die is gain.

'And again I say rejoice'

Some academics repeat themselves a bit too often. Admittedly, they had their one good idea, but it seems that the rest of their career consists in living off the esteem they received for their single contribution, and what is left to them is repeating, restating and rehearsing that one thought. We would do well to avoid rereading them too often.

In his letter to the Philippians Paul repeats himself often too – to such a degree that it becomes almost comical. The repetition is most certainly intended and deliberately executed. In 1:18 we find a repetition within the same sentence, 'I rejoice. … and I will rejoice.' For good measure, this pair is repeated in 2:17 ('I rejoice and I rejoice with you') and again in 2:18 ('Likewise you should rejoice and rejoice with me').[1] The next time Paul even comments on what he is doing: 'rejoice in the Lord. To write the same things to you is no trouble to me and is safe for you' (3:1). By now all readers and listeners will have picked up on the pattern. And then finally we come to 4:4, 'Rejoice in the Lord always; again I will say, Rejoice.' Paul must have enjoyed writing this.

So far we have left out the non-repeated single references to joy: Paul always prays with joy (1:4); he expects to be released from prison for the joy of the Philippians (1:25); the Philippians could make Paul's joy complete by being united in one purpose (2:2); they should welcome back Epaphroditus with great joy (2:29) who has been ill and is keen to come back to the Philippian church; and Paul describes the church in Philippi as his joy in 4:1 (and I have missed at least one).

Yet, despite this repeated emphasis on joy, this letter is not about joy as such but rather about Christ character, the impact of knowing the person of Christ as the one to follow. The letter makes it clear that joy is an unmistakable element of knowing him.

Part of academic enquiry can be negative, trying to test how solid an argument is (either my own or someone else's) and to be sharp, rigorous, penetrating and exact. The academic mind is different from the political mind, which is interested not in the quality of an argument but only in whether it fits a larger agenda (beware of the political mind in academia!). Academics may develop a tendency to test all

1 The same Greek verb, *chairoo*, is used throughout even though the ESV has 'I am glad' (2:17) and 'you … should be glad' (2:18).

statements for their accuracy and truth value (and my wife can testify that this makes for lousy marital conversations).

The academic mind can also experience a lack of joy. I have noticed that people who have embarked on an individual long-haul project (such as a three-year PhD project) struggle more with maintaining this joy than those who have a shorter research-only project. Does the academy at large manage to suck the joy out of these individuals over the years? Does the long grind of working on one thing wear them down? I hope not, but there is a question to be asked, though.

How did Paul rejoice while he was imprisoned and facing potential death, as well as dealing with those who were introducing false doctrine, where we tend to struggle to maintain our joy over three years of research? Paul's reason for joy in this passage moves through two stages. The first is that of the help of fellowship and the second is his own personal expectation of God's future, that all will be for 'deliverance' (1:19), 'salvation' or 'well-being' – all possible translations[2] of that wonderful Greek word *soteria*.

The help that fellowship gives is expressed in the phrase 'through your prayers' (1:19) and quite likely also in the expression 'and the help of the Spirit of Jesus Christ', but there are some difficulties in translating that phrase. Paul knows that things will turn out for his salvation. How? Through their prayers.

We may have picked up the mistaken idea that as academics we live our lives on our own. And then we may give the impression that the successful academic is the solitary thinker who is independently brilliant. But it may not be

2 See H. G. Liddell and R. Scott, *Greek–English Lexicon*, 9th edn, rev. Henry Stuart Jones (Oxford: Clarendon Press, 1996).

true for academics who want to live their lives as Christian academics, who acknowledge that their dependence on the fellowship of the praying community is how they will achieve their goal. The Christian fellowship of which we are part is an essential means by which we find our way through life and work and by which we remain close to the person of Jesus.

The second stage is Paul's vision that all this will be for his deliverance and his salvation. He unpacks this in 1:20: Christ will be honoured; he will be exalted in my body, 'whether by life or by death'. Speaking of not losing sight of the bigger picture, this one is hard to beat. Paul expresses his 'deliverance' (or 'salvation' or 'well-being') in practical terms: he will exalt Christ, whether in life or in death. This radical vision has transformed how Paul faces the serious challenges before him. He has the comfort of seeing things according to first principles. Paul's knowledge of the magnificence of the person of Christ and of his glory and mastery of every situation leads to his decision to magnify Christ in every situation. Put simply, Paul rejoices because he sees the bigger picture – and the bigger picture is Christ.

Back to our long-term researcher who is struggling to maintain their joy. Working on their own, facing mental challenge upon mental challenge, where every bit of attention is sucked up by the problem at hand and problems of time, quality of argument, difficulty in writing and finance, it is all too easy to lose sight of the bigger picture. And for us the bigger picture is Christ.

Every now and then I am asked to write a reference for someone who is applying for a teaching position in a

Christian school. On occasion I have turned this down, namely when the individual has not committed themselves to a local church during their studies or invested themselves in the rough and tumble of the community of believers. What we do in our graduate fellowships or work-based prayer groups is not equivalent to engaging fully in the life of the church even though we may feel more at ease in the former.

It would be wise of us to, like Paul, acknowledge the role of our brothers and sisters, of their prayers and of our accountability to them in maintaining our vision and helping us see the only picture that matters. Paul rejoices, for he knows that Christ will be honoured in life and in death, whether or not with a PhD or a post-doc, in both good circumstances and desperate times – and always, because Paul knows that his vision of the all-sufficiency of Christ is fed and kept alive by the prayer and fellowship of his brothers and sisters. Joy is therefore repeated, and repeated again, many times over.

For further reflection

1 Do you have a group of believers to whom you are accountable and who can help you maintain your joy in living as a follower of Jesus?
2 What are the big issues that threaten to take away your joy as a Christian? Are you able to share these with others so that they can help you in prayer?
3 We saw that the repeated patterns of being somewhere long-term can choke someone's joy. How do we avoid that trap?

Academic exceptionalism

Romans 2:1–11, 17–24

[1]Therefore you have no excuse, O man, every one of you who judges. For in passing judgement on another you condemn yourself, because you, the judge, practise the very same things. [2]We know that the judgement of God rightly falls on those who practise such things. [3]Do you suppose, O man – you who judge those who practise such things and yet do them yourself – that you will escape the judgement of God? [4]Or do you presume on the riches of his kindness and forbearance and patience, not knowing that God's kindness is meant to lead you to repentance? [5]But because of your hard and impenitent heart you are storing up wrath for yourself on the day of wrath when God's righteous judgement will be revealed.

[6]He will render to each one according to his works: [7]to those who by patience in well-doing seek for glory and honour and immortality, he will give eternal life; [8]but for those who are self-seeking and do not obey the truth, but obey unrighteousness, there will be wrath and fury. [9]There will be tribulation and distress for every human being who does evil, the Jew first and also the Greek, [10]but glory and honour and peace for everyone who does good, the Jew first and also the Greek. [11]For God shows no partiality. …

[17]But if you call yourself a Jew and rely on the law and boast in God [18]and know his will and approve what is excellent, because you are instructed from the law; [19]and if you are sure that you yourself are a guide to the blind, a light to those who are in darkness, [20]an instructor of the foolish, a

teacher of children, having in the law the embodiment of knowledge and truth – [21]you then who teach others, do you not teach yourself? While you preach against stealing, do you steal? [22]You who say that one must not commit adultery, do you commit adultery? You who abhor idols, do you rob temples? [23]You who boast in the law dishonour God by breaking the law. [24]For, as it is written, 'The name of God is blasphemed among the Gentiles because of you.'

Do you call yourself an academic?

At this stage in the letter to the Romans, Paul progresses slowly through his argument to demonstrate that the whole world and all of humanity are liable to judgement before God. In this passage he starts a detailed argument to show that it does not make much difference whether you are an ignorant Gentile or a Jew by birth. The latter, of course, stands in the long line of the descendants of Abraham and knows the will of God.

What Paul says is that you may be very good at condemning immoral behaviour as described in that controversial second half of Romans 1, but your condemnation will not benefit you if you are doing the same thing, either directly or indirectly. And, though it takes well into chapter 3 to finish the point, this first stage addresses a weakness that everyone seems to face: we believe that there are good grounds why the rules that are applicable to everyone else do not apply to us, that our specific circumstances excuse us from being subject to the rules that others need to follow.

Here in Romans 2 Paul addresses the issue of exceptionalism, and his method is simple: he just tells his audience that exceptionalism does not work with God: 'you have no excuse' (2:1); 'we know that the judgement of God is according to truth'; 'Do you suppose … that you will escape …?' (2:3); 'He will render to each one' (2:6, KJV); and finally 'God shows no partiality' (2:11). There will be no difference between those who live openly in sin and those who are quick to condemn others and have an unrepentant heart themselves. And, of course, Paul is simply repeating the teaching of Jesus on hypocrisy in different words.

Though the first eleven verses of Chapter 2 simply assume that the knowledge of God's will is used to condemn others, verses 17 to 21 make this explicit: 'you know his will … having in the law the embodiment of knowledge and truth' (2:18, 20). But again, it is of no use to have access to God's truth unless you also obey God's truth.

It may be particularly instructive to have a closer look at verses 3 to 5 in the context of the academy. Let's be fair, if there is one particular enterprise that is exceptional by its very nature, it is research into God's creation and everything in it. And, just as our passage speaks to those who have a better knowledge of Scripture than many others, it also speaks to those of us who have a well-trained mind and enjoy the benefit of working in an environment where we can use our intelligence. We are never far away from a clever and intelligent assessment of whatever question we face. Yet (or, perhaps better, therefore) we are always in danger of thinking that the rules that apply to others do not apply to us: 'Do you suppose, O man – you who judge those who practise such things and yet do them yourself – that you will escape the judgement of God?' (2:3)

What sorts of things do we judge others for while failing to recognise that we are guilty of the very same sins? To start simply – and for an academic close to home (this will apply more to the arts and humanities than to the sciences) – there will be a number of places in our doctoral dissertation where we critique another scholar's work. The criticism may be about faulty logic, ignoring data, shortcomings in the sound weighing of arguments or perhaps something more pernicious. Are we second-guessing the other scholar's agenda (as we perceive it), which may be too liberal or too conservative for our liking? Are our criticisms really justified or might we perhaps be pushing the boundaries of total fairness a tiny bit just for rhetorical effect or to make our point? Are we free from any of the faults we identify in our opponents?

This is about how we do our academic work, but what about bringing the academy into the church? A common complaint is that there is not enough critical thinking in church on an average Sunday. We may think (but would never acknowledge that we do) that the 'common' folk in the pews have their own 'naive' faith, tend to take everything they read at face value and are unaware of the intelligent observations and questions we academics raise when reading Scripture. We may rightfully complain of ignorance in others, but in judging others are we not also judging ourselves? Has our learning perhaps made us look more important without any gain at all? Some might ask if we have become puffed up. But, to return to the early verses of Romans 2, are we ignorant that one day we shall stand before God's throne and give an account of everything we have said, whether about the work of another scholar or about the people of God in our church?

When we took our dog to dog school, we learned that the time between the sinful act and punishment should be as short as possible. Then I had children. When they were relatively young there was still some truth in this principle, but the older they got the less well it worked (some would say the less anything works).

With God, there is a considerable time between sin and judgement. This interval is characterised by three words: 'kindness', 'forbearance' and 'patience'. When God delays his judgement on our brazen judging of others, it is a sign of his mercy. He shows this kindness with the express goal of bringing us to repentance for our presumptions. We have made up our mind, we have accepted the ruling paradigms of our discipline and we are ready to make high claims. Yet Scripture says: 'do you presume on the riches of his kindness and forbearance and patience, not knowing that God's kindness is meant to lead you to repentance?' (2:4). Do we realise that God's kindness is meant to lead us to repentance? The freedom we have, the kindness we experience and the apparent delay before the time of judgement are a time of patience for repentance, so that we might seek what is truly honourable, good and immortal. Therefore, we pray that the next verse will never be true for us: 'But because of your hard and impenitent heart you are storing up wrath for yourself on the day of wrath when God's righteous judgement will be revealed' (2:5).

It is quite a sobering statement, that we could be in the process of storing up wrath against that final day. Yet there is a wonderful balancing phrase in this verse, a promise in disguise, 'because of your hard and impenitent heart'. The ultimate killer is the direction in which our heart is set. What will it be – a stubborn and unrepentant heart or an overwhelming notion of God's kindness, forbearance and patience – that leads us to repentance? Will we take his word and his church for what they truly are, namely his?

Let our prayer today be a moment in which we arrest our private notions of exceptionalism, of claiming a special position as enlightened academics, and ask our Father to remove anything that is stubborn and unrepentant.

For further reflection

1 As academics we do not simply acquire knowledge but we also develop skills in evaluation of arguments, reading well and engaging in complex thought. How do we use these skills for good in the church? Is it at all possible to use such skills in the church without offending the leadership or creating envy? Be brutally honest with yourself!
2 Is it a waste of your talents if the church does not make use of your academic skills?
3 How much of a divide is there between your academic intelligence and your spiritual intelligence? Are you cleverer in your academic speciality than in your spiritual life?

Intelligent reading

Romans 8:31–39

[31]What then shall we say to these things? If God is for us, who can be against us? [32]He who did not spare his own Son but gave him up for us all, how will he not also with him graciously give us all things? [33]Who shall bring any charge against God's elect? It is God who justifies. [34]Who is to condemn? Christ Jesus is the one who died – more than that, who was raised – who is at the right hand of God, who indeed is interceding for us. [35]Who shall separate us from the love of Christ? Shall tribulation, or distress, or persecution, or famine, or nakedness, or danger, or sword? [36]As it is written,

> 'For your sake we are being killed all the day long;
> we are regarded as sheep to be slaughtered.'

[37]No, in all these things we are more than conquerors through him who loved us. [38]For I am sure that neither death nor life, nor angels nor rulers, nor things present nor things to come, nor powers, [39]nor height nor depth, nor anything else in all creation, will be able to separate us from the love of God in Christ Jesus our Lord.

'Who is to condemn?'

If you have made it this far, you will have picked up on what we are trying to do. Instead of quick one-thought devotionals, we are digging into the Bible to see how it addresses issues we face as academics. Many of you may come from backgrounds where the ministry to postgrads and postdocs goes beyond what I had known before I came to Cambridge. My experience was that I was rarely addressed as a Christian within the academy. Yet we need to let Scripture ask questions of us. The Bible should function like a two-edged sword that dissects our hidden thoughts and ambitions, sometimes to encourage and sometimes to show us a painful shortcoming in our life.

But not all questions are painful. On the contrary, questions sometimes take over when we run out of superlatives. Who is a god like our God? Or, like 8:31, where the underlying sentiment of the first question is something like 'Can we add anything? Is there anything more glorious to say?' Rhetorical questions take over when our mind has run out of words, whether in our deepest delight or in our darkest misery.

Romans 8:31–39 is well known, and I hope that even just reading the passage will feel like coming home to a warm place that cheers the heart. The passage forms the capstone of an argument that Paul started back in chapter 1, which traces how God overcomes the sin and futility of the world. God is righteous even when he acquits the sinner. Moreover, he makes our mortal bodies alive by the Spirit that he has given us, and by the time we reach 8:31 the path to complete salvation has been explained in its full glory.

In Romans, more than anywhere else, Paul drives his argument forwards by means of questions that are intended to keep the reader actively involved, to draw us in so that we become part of the thought process. These rhetorical questions invite us to immerse ourselves mentally and emotionally in Paul's explanation of the central place of faith as the way to enjoy God's salvation. And there are at least five of these questions in our passage.

The first question in Romans 8:31 is a bit of a filler: 'What then shall we say to these things?' This is the fifth of a total of seven questions in the letter to the Romans that start with 'What then shall we say …?' In this case, there is no change of direction or tackling of a further objection. What follows is sheer exultation. Is there anything more to say?

The second and third questions belong together because they both share the same premise, that God is on our side: 'If God is for us, who can be against us?' (8:31b). The words 'God is for us' are then unpacked in 8:32, where God's acts are further described in two clauses: 'he who did not spare his own Son' and he who 'gave him up for us all'. How will this God not give us everything with his Son? Incidentally, this is one of the few verses where we get the two terms 'for us' and 'with him' in a single sentence: substitution (he died for us) and union with Christ (we died with him) melded in a question of sheer joy in the truth of God.

Without interruption the next question is asked: 'Who shall bring any charge …?' (8:33). And the following words are not a direct answer, though initially they may be read as such. The thought is that no one can bring an accusation when it is God who justifies. Note that the correct interpretation does not come from any grammatical marking of the rhetorical question or the explanation that follows, but simply from the meaning of the words. If it is *God* who justifies, no accusation will stand.

The next question needs to be taken in similar vein: 'Who is to condemn?' (8:34). Again, the following words are not a direct answer. The point is not that Christ will condemn but instead that there is no condemnation because Christ is the one who died and, what is more, the one who was raised and is therefore at the right hand of God, where he intercedes for us. Knowing this, who can condemn while he is actively working for our benefit?

Then in 8:35 Paul asks the fifth question. Here the meaning of the text again overrides the formal conventions of grammar. The question, which is of course again rhetorical: 'Who shall separate us from the love of Christ?' In Greek writing there was no question mark till the eighth century AD or so, and normally a question would be indicated by a word such as 'who', 'what' or 'where' or made clear otherwise.

So we have the question, 'Who shall separate us from the love of Christ?' In a strictly formal interpretation, the words that follow might be read as the answer to the question – at least if you are not in the same place of exultation as the apostle Paul is – because what follows in the Greek is simply a list of nouns connected by 'or' (the translators have added the word 'shall' and the question mark). What shall separate us? 'Tribulation, or distress, or persecution, or famine, or nakedness, or danger, or sword?' Grammatically, there is no reason not to see this as an answer to the preceding question, but, using the same phrase again, if you are where the apostle Paul is – in a place of sheer delight in the unimaginable blessings of being saved by Jesus – it is unthinkable that anything could separate us, and therefore we also need to read this list of nouns with a question mark after them (as every translation duly does). No, none of these things can separate us from the love of Christ. And, for good measure, Paul adds loads of other things in 8:38–39 that are equally unable to separate us from the love of God in Christ Jesus our Lord. Death, life, angels, rulers, present things, things to come, powers, height, depth, 'anything else in all creation' (this last term may have been added for those who feel that their favourite bogeyman has been left out). What can separate us? Having absorbed eight chapters of God's salvation, we ought to respond, 'Surely nothing!'

Two points to bring this home to where we are. First, why does Paul mention specific items such as hardships, distress, persecution and famine? The answer is, of course, that by instinct we fear that these things might separate us from his love. We are scared of hardship, persecution, illness or being unemployed and unable to provide for our family. These things can keep us awake at night. We think that they can harm us too easily and separate us from God's loving care and provision. Yet at this point in the letter the pastoral message is quite simple. Given the outpouring of grace and compassion, and victory in the Spirit, how could we do anything other than trust that God will most certainly give us everything with Christ? Though the whole list in 8:38 is supposed to be a list of things that *cannot* separate us, yet too often we treat hardships as if they *do* separate us and we fear them.

Second, looking at the grammar of this text in an analytical and dispassionate way, we could get the passage hopelessly wrong. If we are not in the same place of delight in God's salvation as Paul, it is just about possible that we can mess up the text. The way some of the questions are followed by words that are not a direct answer can trip us up in reading the passage without preparation. To arrive at the right reading, we need to have internalised the argument.

This potential misreading of the questions and answers here in Romans 8 is a good illustration of what can go wrong when we read the Bible. If we read its words without internalising its message and without acknowledging the reality of God and his interventions in this world, we will fail to notice its logic and coherence. Scripture asks to be read with a mindset that is sympathetic to its goals.

And that is where the community of believers comes in. When we are stuck with a list of nouns and cannot see the forest for the trees, we need others to come together and pray, correct and encourage, and worship the living God. That every research project should start with a question may or may not be true but I believe that true Christian research into any aspect of reality will end where Paul finishes in our passage, with questions that express a deep commitment to the amazing provision and glory of the God who created, sustains and redeems his people.

For further reflection

1 Where do you see the greatness of God in your research?
2 Romans 8:36 suggests that various hardships are an integral part of the life of the believer. How does the whole passage help us to see God's goodness through these hardships?
3 When you see the phrase 'community of believers', do you think of your church or another gathering? If nothing comes to mind, how could you move towards a 'community of believers'?

Divine interventions

Acts 1:1–11

[1]In the first book, O Theophilus, I have dealt with all that Jesus began to do and teach, [2]until the day when he was taken up, after he had given commands through the Holy Spirit to the apostles whom he had chosen. [3]He presented himself alive to them after his suffering by many proofs, appearing to them during forty days and speaking about the kingdom of God.

[4]And while staying with them he ordered them not to depart from Jerusalem, but to wait for the promise of the Father, which, he said, 'you heard from me; [5]for John baptized with water, but you will be baptized with the Holy Spirit not many days from now.'

[6]So when they had come together, they asked him, 'Lord, will you at this time restore the kingdom to Israel?' [7]He said to them, 'It is not for you to know times or seasons that the Father has fixed by his own authority. [8]But you will receive power when the Holy Spirit has come upon you, and you will be my witnesses in Jerusalem and in all Judea and Samaria, and to the end of the earth.' [9]And when he had said these things, as they were looking on, he was lifted up, and a cloud took him out of their sight. [10]And while they were gazing into heaven as he went, behold, two men stood by them in white robes, [11]and said, 'Men of Galilee, why do you stand looking into heaven? This Jesus, who was taken up from you into heaven, will come in the same way as you saw him go into heaven.'

'It is not for you to know'

Being engaged in academia is a tricky business. When we signed up to do research in the context of the secular academy, we committed ourselves to engage in a conversation that involves participants of various persuasions: there are Christians and non-Christians, sceptics, minimalists, the orthodox, the neo-orthodox, the traditional and the progressive, theists, atheists and agnostics. Academic conversation has certain rules that both enable the conversation to take place and limit the things that can be said. In our research we study the things that can be described in terms of observable and natural reality. This results in the strangest of possible ironies: as Christians we are committed to talk about the result of God's direct interventions in this world in terms that avoid using his intervention as the ultimate cause of the events.

This plays out differently in different disciplines. A Christian neuroscientist has to struggle with a discipline that can study only what is observed, without using the biblical revelation on the human spirit or even the possibility of the indwelling of the Holy Spirit as an explanation. Physicists deal with all sorts of phenomena in created reality but have so far failed to observe the great cause of reality, an intelligent God, or to detect spiritual beings such as demons or angels, who appear in this passage. A Christian physicist may know that God and spiritual beings are part of reality, but how and where lie pretty much outside the field. We have a concept of reality that is bigger than what we study on a day-to-day basis.

This passage mentions some out-of-this-world phenomena: two angels talking to the disciples and also Jesus being taken up into heaven in the most extraordinary way. If the Gospel of Luke has not already convinced us that, to understand Jesus, we need a perspective that is bigger than just the natural and the repeatable, most certainly Luke's second book rubs it in from the very beginning. Jesus was dead, came back to life and was taken up to heaven. The divine activity in this world is explicit, and if we do not accept this, the Gospel will remain a mystery.

Given this context, we are set up to consider the question raised by the disciples in 1:6: 'Lord, will you at this time restore the kingdom to Israel?' The question is about things to come (the technical term is 'eschatology'). Given that God worked actively, visibly and miraculously in Jesus Christ, and that God is working today mainly in a more concealed and therefore, incidentally, a culturally more acceptable way, the question is whether there will be a time when direct public intervention will resume. For the disciples the question is also a political one. When will he, who is the Son of David, take the throne of David in the city of David?

Luke likes to record these eschatological questions. In his first book, he records this: 'Being asked by the Pharisees when the kingdom of God would come, [Jesus] answered them, "The kingdom of God is not coming with signs to be observed, nor will they say, 'Look, here it is!' or 'There!' for behold, the kingdom of God is in the midst of you"' (Luke 17:20–21). A little later, Jesus tells them 'a parable, because he was near to Jerusalem, and because they supposed that the kingdom of God was to appear immediately' (Luke 19:11). This is the parable of the ten minas and the citizens who did not want the man of noble birth to be king over them. Again, in reply to Jesus's remark that not one stone will be left on top of another, the disciples ask, 'when will these things be, and what will be the sign when these things are about to take place?' (Luke 21:7), to which part of the answer is that 'Jerusalem will be trampled underfoot by the Gentiles, until the times of the Gentiles are fulfilled' (Luke 21:24).

By Acts 1, the disciples have learned something about the kingdom of God and perhaps concluded that the Gentiles have trampled all over Jerusalem and killed the representative of God's people, the Christ himself, and that the kingdom of God has been established in the resurrection. So the question the disciples ask is a valid one. Now that the kingdom of God is here in all its resurrection force, now that the promise of the Father is coming soon (1:4), will the kingdom be restored to Israel?

What I like about this question is that the disciples remain firmly focused on actual events in the real world, not something vague such as an eschatology based on an obscure and vaguely expressed hope that the kingdom will be built slowly. Instead, they are asking about a down-to-earth physical and visible intervention by God.

Jesus's answer addresses only the issue of timing, 'It is not for you to know times or seasons' (1:6). The how of restoring the kingdom to Israel has been dwelled on before and does not need elaboration, even though the angels ensure that they remind the disciples – and us – of that earlier teaching. The question of when and 'how long' remains unanswered. There are things that remain unrevealed.

The Cambridge college of which I am a member has a statement that is read out when someone is incorporated, and it contains the sentence: 'Knowledge should be the possession of all.' By and large, I agree. But universal knowledge is certainly not a human right. There is knowledge that is too big for us to carry around, even for us academics. God keeps things to himself. Why? I don't know. I can speculate but ultimately I don't know. Yet, since I believe that God is good, I trust that he has a good reason for it. Not all is revealed and there are limits to what can be known.

The blatant supernaturalism of Luke is alien to today's general cultural and intellectual life. That not everything can be known is equally offensive. By the end of the book of Acts, after a long series of rejections by various leaders of the Jews both in Jerusalem and at the ends of the earth (in Rome), we know the answer to the question that was asked: the kingdom has not been restored to Israel during the time covered by the book of Acts.

The history of the early church plays out in a world where God has been at work and will be at work. And the apostles receive a concrete task in the midst of all this: 'you will be my witnesses' (1:8).

We can justifiably read ourselves into the story at this point. We work and live in a context that is based on different principles from what God had intended. We do our academic work in an environment where knowledge that is valued is not based on revelation but on human ingenuity. And in this environment Jesus says, 'you will be my witnesses'. How? The answer to this question has been revealed. We are to be witnesses of Jesus through the power of the Holy Spirit, through the promise of the Father, who lives in the heart of every believer.

For further reflection

1. Is it possible to hold a naturalist worldview in our academic work at the same time as we hold a supernatural worldview in our life of faith without the two ever colliding? How healthy is it to have two separate worldviews?
2. In much of our academic work we accept a methodological naturalism, that is, we are looking for explanations that do not need direct divine intervention. At what point does a methodological naturalism fall short?
3. Are God's public supernatural interventions in the past and the future a stumbling block for evangelism? Or are they a powerful means for drawing people in?

Pedagogy

Acts 8:26–40

[26]Now an angel of the Lord said to Philip, 'Rise and go
toward the south to the road that goes down from Jerusalem
to Gaza.' This is a desert place. [27]And he rose and went.
And there was an Ethiopian, a eunuch, a court official of
Candace, queen of the Ethiopians, who was in charge of all
her treasure. He had come to Jerusalem to worship [28]and
was returning, seated in his chariot, and he was reading
the prophet Isaiah. [29]And the Spirit said to Philip, 'Go over
and join this chariot.' [30]So Philip ran to him and heard him
reading Isaiah the prophet and asked, 'Do you understand
what you are reading?' [31]And he said, 'How can I, unless
someone guides me?' And he invited Philip to come up and
sit with him. [32]Now the passage of the Scripture that he was
reading was this:

'Like a sheep he was led to the slaughter
 and like a lamb before its shearer is silent,
 so he opens not his mouth.
[33]In his humiliation justice was denied him.
 Who can describe his generation?
For his life is taken away from the earth.'

[34]And the eunuch said to Philip, 'About whom, I ask you,
does the prophet say this, about himself or about someone
else?' [35]Then Philip opened his mouth, and beginning with
this Scripture he told him the good news about Jesus. [36]And
as they were going along the road they came to some water,
and the eunuch said, 'See, here is water! What prevents me

from being baptized?' [38]And he commanded the chariot to stop, and they both went down into the water, Philip and the eunuch, and he baptized him. [39]And when they came up out of the water, the Spirit of the Lord carried Philip away, and the eunuch saw him no more, and went on his way rejoicing. [40]But Philip found himself at Azotus, and as he passed through he preached the gospel to all the towns until he came to Caesarea.

Let someone guide me

The story of the court official from Ethiopia is one of the passages of Scripture that should be a particular delight for anyone involved in education. What is better than teaching a keen student who is asking all the right questions? When it comes to biblical role models for us educators, there are some negative examples, such as the teachers of the law. In contrast, the special role given to Philip in explaining the gospel, starting from a promising passage of the Bible, is something any Christian teacher will embrace.

The story has four actors, the Ethiopian and Philip being the two obvious ones. But right at the start there is also a direct intervention by an angel of the Lord who instructs Philip where to go (8:26). Later this role is taken by a fourth actor, the Holy Spirit, who tells Philip what to do (8:29). We hardly notice the change from angel to Spirit: both are regular voices that guide the faithful. At the end, it is the Holy Spirit again who carries Philip away from the scene (8:39). There seems to be a large overlap in the types of things the Holy Spirit and the angel do.

The more prominent character is Philip. He is simply called Philip, without any further description or disambiguation.

This is the same Philip who was preaching in Samaria earlier in the chapter (8:5) and must be the same Philip who is one of the seven deacons appointed in Acts 6:5. This Philip is not the same Philip as Philip the apostle, mentioned in Acts 1. Clearly the reputation of this Philip in the early church was such that simply 'Philip', rather than 'Philip the evangelist' or 'Philip the deacon', is sufficient to avoid confusion with Philip the apostle. There is no need for Philip the deacon to fret about having missed out on being an apostle or to be envious of people higher up the hierarchy. At least within the narrative of Acts, this Philip eclipses the other Philip. And this Philip is told to go to a desert road, which is not the place where one would meet many people, and he awaits further instructions.

The remaining actor is, of course, the Ethiopian, the eunuch, a court official of Candace (8:27). In the remainder of the story he is not called 'the Ethiopian', as he is the first time, but 'the eunuch'. The standard designation for him is the 'eunuch' (8:34, 36, 38, 39); the most jarring feature of this man's existence is the way he is referred to, which emphasises how he is different, with all its physical and hormonal consequences.[1] On visits to the Temple he would be kept at a distance, in line with the law of Moses (Deuteronomy 23:1). A law such as this feels unfair, especially in our current context, which emphasises inclusion. The point, however, is that God makes clear that no one is allowed before him because we all fall short of his glory (Romans 3:23). In the Temple only the high priest, briefly and once

1 Jean D. Wilson and Claus Roehrborn, 'Long-term Consequences of Castration in Men: Lessons from the Skoptzy and Eunuchs of the Chinese and Ottoman Courts', *Journal of Clinical Endocrinology & Metabolism* 84 (1999): 4324–31.

a year, was able to appear in the most holy place. Still, the eunuch had a disadvantage and quite probably a visible one.

So, in line with the biblical terminology, let's identify him by his physical status. The eunuch is a high official and probably an intelligent man, given the type of questions he is asking. He is also travelling quite comfortably, given that he is able to read while riding in a chariot (think Rolls-Royce rather than an old rust bucket), so we can assume that he is wealthy.

This eunuch is reading Isaiah, when he finds himself suddenly on a desert road with a man running beside the chariot who asks him, 'Do you understand what you are reading?' (8:31). The eunuch must think this to be a remarkable coincidence. Right when he is thinking that Scripture is hard to understand, out of nowhere a man appears, picking up on a thought he has just had. What a coincidence!

Of course, it was no such thing. Our heavenly Father goes to great lengths to organise events to bring people close to him. In this instance, the veil on this hidden activity is lifted briefly. Angels are involved; the Spirit talks to a believer, a Christian who has to walk into nowhere and is then told to run towards a chariot, all perfectly timed. Life is not random.

Philip has taken the initiative, having been prompted by both the angel and the Spirit. The eunuch so happens to be reading what we now call Isaiah 53 (there were no chapter numbers in those days). Isaiah 53 is only a few chapters before Isaiah 56, which talks about eunuchs (keep this thought for a moment).

The eunuch answers with words that not only every teacher but every Christian loves to hear, 'How can I, unless someone guides me?' (8:31). It is music to our ears! But how often do we actually hear these words? How often do we encounter such keenness for our insights? Is there perhaps space for a complaint that the church is not asking us often enough, that they are losing interest in us and therefore in the very intellectual life to which we have devoted ourselves? Might this lack of desire for our insights perhaps be a partial explanation for why academics tend to be a bit pessimistic about the state of the church's intellectual life? (I hope you get that I am saying this tongue in cheek.)

The eunuch follows up with the insightful question as to whether the prophet speaks of himself or of someone else (8:34). Now Luke, as the narrator of the story, does something interesting. In the cited words from Isaiah, the lamb does not open his mouth (8:32). What is the first thing that Philip does? He opens his mouth (8:35). The image from Isaiah is reversed to show that the time of silence has passed: the full gospel is now preached openly.

Philip starts with Isaiah and from there he preaches Jesus Christ (8:35): how Jesus willingly suffered great injustice to the point of death and how he healed us; how he took our punishment and obtained for us a non-guilty verdict in the cosmic courtroom of God's judgement; and how Jesus brings us into the most holy place, because in him our sin and our ugliness have all been done away with.

The story develops rapidly from here. The eunuch sees water (another coincidence) and wants to be baptised (8:36). Philip baptises him and disappears from the scene (8:39). There is no dramatic climax, and we are left to ponder what happens afterwards.

The first thing to note is that Philip does not receive any public credit for what he does. Unlike the structures in the academy, which acknowledge our achievements, Philip is simply carried away by the Spirit. He is, of course, presented as an example. He is willing to go to desert places, to put the hard work in, to open conversations and answer questions, and to be taken away while there is still so much to share. Philip is the ideal Christian intellectual, who is willing to preach Christ and to listen to the angel and to the Spirit.

The second thing is about teaching strategy. Obviously Luke is aware of Isaiah 56:3–5:

> 'let not the eunuch say,
>   Behold, I am a dry tree.'
> For thus says the LORD:
> '… I will give in my house and within my walls
>   a monument and a name
> better than sons and daughters;
> I will give them an everlasting name
>   that shall not be cut off …'

Yet, Philip is not described as mentioning these verses to the eunuch, nor does Luke alert his readers to this passage, even though it is screaming from the pages of our Bible to be noticed. He leaves out the obvious because he is a great teacher. A teacher leaves space for discovery, for the student's joy in making stunning discoveries, for transformative bursts of insight. Imagine what the eunuch must be thinking as he continues to read Isaiah 53 and slowly makes his way through Isaiah 54 ('What a great image of the barren woman who becomes the mother of many'), then Isaiah 55 ('I was the one who was thirsty for true water but have now returned to the Lord'), to arrive at Isaiah 56, where the Lord gives him a place in his house better than that of sons and daughters. Imagine his eyes light up when he sees Scripture address his own situation: 'That is me!'

It has been the experience of many Christians to be personally addressed by the word of God. This is the power of Scripture and we should expect it to happen. Being a Christian academic is not about being part of an elite of learned show-offs. Rather, it is about people who grow in their understanding so that, when they read on in their journey, they suddenly recognise themselves: 'That's me: that is Scripture talking about who I am in Christ!'

For further reflection

1. How is Philip an example?
2. This passage in the Bible is about reading the Bible. What do we learn about the various ways in which the words of Isaiah function in this story (i.e. Isaiah 53 quoted and Isaiah 56 present in the background)?
3. What difference does it make to our everyday lives knowing that God is actively directing events and encounters?

The household code and our weak spots

Colossians 3:17 – 4:2

[17]And whatever you do, in word or deed, do everything in
the name of the Lord Jesus, giving thanks to God the Father
through him.
[18]Wives, submit to your husbands, as is fitting in the Lord.
[19]Husbands, love your wives, and do not be harsh with them.
[20]Children, obey your parents in everything, for this pleases
the Lord.
[21]Fathers, do not provoke your children, lest they become
discouraged. [22]Slaves, obey in everything those who are your
earthly masters, not by way of eye-service, as people-pleasers,
but with sincerity of heart, fearing the Lord. [23]Whatever you
do, work heartily, as for the Lord and not for men, [24]knowing
that from the Lord you will receive the inheritance as your
reward. You are serving the Lord Christ. [25]For the wrong-
doer will be paid back for the wrong he has done, and there
is no partiality.
[4:1]Masters, treat your slaves justly and fairly, knowing that
you also have a Master in heaven.
[2]Continue steadfastly in prayer, being watchful in it with
thanksgiving.

'As is fitting in the Lord'

Colossians is not a particularly easy letter. It has described the supremacy of Christ who is the first of creation (1:15) and holds all things together (1:17). There have been warnings against a false intellectualism (2:8) and an exposition of how the Christian life is about taking off the old person (3:9) and putting on the new (3:12). And then we come to this passage, which may feel like a step down from the heights of Christology to the messiness of our family life. From the excellence of Christ in old and new creation to the frustrations of parenthood. There is something safe about the wonderful theological vistas of the earlier part of the letter. We can meditate on being crucified with Christ (2:20) and on being hidden with Christ in heaven (3:3), but now we descend from the peaks of theology to the so-called household code. Our everyday life as spouses, parents and waged servants is not always connected with the things we believe. Our closest relationships are often messy. We preach that Christ is lord over everything but in practice we make exceptions for ourselves, our family and our life as an employer or employee. That part of our life gets under our skin and can cause serious frustration.

What is the context of our passage? Earlier in the letter we were told: 'seek the things that are above' (3:1); 'Set your minds on things that are above' (3:2); 'your life is hidden with Christ in God' (3:3); 'you have put off the old self … and have put on the new self' (3:9–10). But how does this lofty language work in practice?

The household code is an intentional part of the letter. It is framed by references to prayer and to thanksgiving (3:17; 4:2). Colossians is full of thanksgiving (1:3; 1:12; 2:7; 3:15–16), and it is not difficult to see why. The basic argument is that Christ is the head of all and the one in whom we have been reconciled with God. And we are united with the head of everything in such a way that Paul can say that we are in him and he in us. Christ has made the new life possible; we have received everything in him. There is only one reaction possible and that is thanksgiving.

This passage contains three pairs of commands: to wives and husbands, to children and fathers, and to slaves and masters. Only in the final pair does gender not play a role.

As Paul is talking about daily life, it is not surprising that there is an emphasis on Jesus as lord. After all, a lord directs the lives of those belonging to him. For this reason, 3:17 uses the expression 'in the name of the Lord Jesus'. The next verse talks about what is 'fitting in the Lord' (3:18) and 3:20 about what 'pleases the Lord'. There are four references to the Lord in 3:22–24, and the 'Master' in heaven translates the same word (Greek *kurios*). Before and after this passage the term 'Christ' is used to refer to the Lord Jesus Christ, which makes the use of 'Lord' in these verses all the more meaningful.

One way to understand these commands to married couples, fathers and children, and slaves and masters is to see them as addressing the one area where it is easiest to stumble, that is, Paul addresses our greatest weakness in each of these relationships. This means that for a husband a weak spot is not to love his wife but instead to be harsh with her. The weak spot of a father is to provoke his children to the point of discouraging them. What is true of the relation between masters and slaves may, by extension, be applied to modern employment relationships, laying bare some of the critical danger zones in this area.

When Paul addresses us in this way, he brings out something that makes us uncomfortable. We do not like our weak spots to be pointed out, especially in the relationships that are a large part of our life.

It is good to reflect on some of the specific challenges academics face in these areas. One such area is the strains and stresses that academic work can place on a marriage. Sometimes we joke about our current book or dissertation as 'our baby', one with an unusually long gestation period. In practice, a dissertation can be loved more than the child that is born during the PhD process, but more often it functions as an extramarital affair. Our academic work should not be either a child or a lover.

The workplace, with its curious mix of relationships with unequal power dynamics, can be a source of endless frustration. Paul highlights the moral obligations of an employer or supervisor to an employee, and of an employee towards our Lord in heaven. We often find it difficult to see the pain and frustration we experience in our departments in terms of the lordship of Jesus because it gives short shrift to our sense of entitlement when we feel unjustly treated. It is tempting as an employee to cut corners in our hours and commitment when we feel that our employer is doing the same to us.

But the relationship that is true for most of us is that between children and their parents. Our parents have had an enormous influence on our lives. I have seen more than one scholar driven by their reaction to an abusive or neglectful father, who had long since passed away. This would raise the stakes when a research question was formulated and created an intense need to be right that went beyond normal scholarly debate. How far do you feel your parents still looking over your shoulder, judging and criticising your work (and it does not make a difference whether they are still alive)? Is there unfinished business in our relationships with our parents? Don't make your academic work an excuse for not pleasing the Lord in this area of life.

Besides the complications of past hurts and difficult relationships, there is the real problem of being away from our parents while we are working on a PhD. It is difficult to look after them when we are in a different country, but we should still make every effort to keep in touch via phone calls, by sending pictures and by giving them attention. My parents, who lived in the Netherlands, are no longer alive but they have weighed most on me while I was living and working in the United Kingdom. When we are low on energy, it is so easy to abdicate our responsibility as children.

To those of us who have children: our work, our book or our dissertation is not our baby, even though we may give it more love and attention than our actual children. None of our children deserve to share their status with pixels on a screen or blobs of ink on a page. For those who don't have children, think of the friends and family you love: are they not more valuable than your work?

Christ is our Lord in heaven. He is everything and all the fullness of God dwells in him. We have been given a place with him. He is our life; he is our hope of glory; he is our present and our future. As we put off the old self and put on the new self, like our Lord we are restored in becoming image-bearers of the invisible God. Thanks be to him who made us wives or husbands, children, parents, supervisors or employees. Thanks to our Lord Jesus that he is lord over all this and that we are called to please him in everything.

For further reflection

1. How does the lordship of Jesus play out in your life?
2. Relationships can sometimes be strained. What are the best examples of Lord-pleasing relationships you have in your life and in your work?
3. What are the weak spots in the various relationships you have?

Reading Scripture

Deuteronomy 17:14–20

[14]When you come to the land that the Lord your God is giving you, and you possess it and dwell in it and then say, 'I will set a king over me, like all the nations that are around me,' [15]you may indeed set a king over you whom the Lord your God will choose. One from among your brothers you shall set as king over you. You may not put a foreigner over you, who is not your brother. [16]Only he must not acquire many horses for himself or cause the people to return to Egypt in order to acquire many horses, since the Lord has said to you, 'You shall never return that way again.' [17]And he shall not acquire many wives for himself, lest his heart turn away, nor shall he acquire for himself excessive silver and gold.

[18]And when he sits on the throne of his kingdom, he shall write for himself in a book a copy of this law, approved by the Levitical priests. [19]And it shall be with him, and he shall read in it all the days of his life, that he may learn to fear the Lord his God by keeping all the words of this law and these statutes, and doing them, [20]that his heart may not be lifted up above his brothers, and that he may not turn aside from the commandment, either to the right hand or to the left, so that he may continue long in his kingdom, he and his children, in Israel.

'That he may learn to fear the LORD'

One of the great slogans that has echoed down the centuries from the Protestant Reformation is the Latin phrase *sola scriptura*, 'Scripture alone'.[1] It acknowledges that Scripture, as the word of God, has supreme authority. The passages in the Bible that speak about the actual reading of Scripture tell us something about how the Bible is to function in the life of the believer. Deuteronomy 17 contains stipulations for future kings of Israel. After mentioning the selection criteria for such a king and some of the things that he should avoid, the text turns in 17:18 to our topic, which is the role of Scripture. It starts with a most remarkable instruction: the king is expected to write out his own copy of the law. Not only does this assume that he is able to read and write, which is interesting in itself, but it also tells us how the law is to be used. It is there to be copied and shared so that it extends beyond the sphere of the Levites. The English Standard Version translation says that this copy has to be 'approved by the Levitical priests' (17:18), but a more literal rendering would be 'from before the Levitical priests'. That the king's copy must be approved suggests that the Levites have to check the king's copy, which makes sense. After all, the king should not be left with a deficient copy that may be missing a section through carelessness. However, 'from before' could also mean that the Levites have the master scroll, which functions as an exemplar for the royal copy, a direct descendant of the original text. That these Levites were in charge of the original becomes clear in Deuteronomy 31,

1 The expression had already been used by Martin Luther in 1520, but its use in the systematic summary of the five main points of the Reformation is more recent.

where Moses entrusts the book of the law to the Levites who carry the ark (Deuteronomy 31:24–26).

Intriguing though this remark about scribal culture is, in the next verse we read how this copy is to be used: 'And it shall be with him, and he shall read in it all the days of his life' (17:19). God stipulates that the reading of Scripture is not a privilege of the religious class or clergy; the king is expected to read it for himself. The biblical scholars in the form of Levitical priests are instrumental in preserving and demonstrating what the law is about, but they are not to stand between the king and his own exposure to God's word.

The result of this lifelong reading will be first, that the king will learn to fear the Lord (17:19). The goal is not to learn political theology, but rather to foster a personal relationship with the Lord himself: 'to fear the LORD his God'. It is a natural and practical consequence that the king expresses the fear of the Lord through 'keeping the words and to do them' (17:19). Some of us may have gotten all excited when we were talking about copying manuscripts – it is my own academic field. However, keeping the law is not about preserving a manuscript but about doing what it says.

The fear of the Lord prevents two things from happening. The first is so 'that his heart may not be lifted up above his brothers' (17:20). The second is to prevent straying from the law to the left or the right, which means keeping the law. This whole section finishes with the promise of a long reign over the children of God.

These commands for the king are a special application of the repeated call in Deuteronomy to study the word, meditate on it and fully live it, from early morning to late evening, to put it on the doorposts and between our eyes, to teach our children, to talk about it when walking and sitting down (Deuteronomy 6:6–9).

The importance of someone's words is commensurate with the importance of the speaker. Few of us will dispute that God is the most important person ever to have spoken, and that makes his word the most important word ever. It makes the king a mere student, who has to sit down, transcribe, read and meditate on the words of God, whose position is much higher than his. This passage ranks the authority and prestige of the word firmly above that of the king.

In the academy we have experience of the concept of authoritative knowledge, but it is not knowledge produced by the words of the highest authority. Rather, it is the result of research, of experiments or of careful arguing. Which does not prime us to accept Scripture as something that rises above our usual definition of true knowledge. But now that we are conscious of this tension, what are its implications for our work?

First, the fear of God is both the beginning of knowledge and wisdom and the result of exposure to his word. It is so easy to lose that fear, to narrow the scope of the type of knowledge we are interested in to just our thesis or current project and to lose sight of the knowledge that has come to us by revelation.

Second, there is also the demand that the word of God is not just treated as an intellectual exercise, but more importantly as a word to be acted on. The king has a position of power and prestige, and studying the word was needed to keep him humble among his brothers. Not every humble person on this world is a listener to God's word, but every listener who does God's word is humble. The revelation of God corrects any idea we might have that all true knowledge is produced by research.

Third, we ought to ask ourselves: am I turning to the right or to the left of God's word? Am I going astray somewhere? Be open to being corrected when you are apt to forget whose world we are studying, when you think that there is nothing beyond natural causes, when you create an intellectual world that has no God. Because these things happen when we fail to listen to the full and complete word of God, day and night, from getting up in the morning to bedtime at night.

And, finally, *sola scriptura* ('Scripture alone') makes sense if we know who has spoken or who is still speaking. It is good to remind ourselves that no commentary or devotional is or can be a substitute for reading Scripture. And our research-produced knowledge can never replace God's own word. Important though the king, the scholar and the scientist are, we are reduced to mere school kids before the life-bringing word of the Father.

For further reflection

1 Meditating on Scripture is often difficult because through the day we have exhausted the same part of our brain carrying out our academic work. What are some practical ways to address this conflict? How can we help one another?
2 Which parts of the Bible are most precious to you? Which parts do you find most difficult to accept?
3 'For whatever was written in former days was written for our instruction, that through endurance and

through the encouragement of the Scriptures we might have hope' (Romans 15:4). In what ways do these words reflect your own experience? How do they help us to better understand reading the Bible?

Epilogue

In the previous nineteen chapters we have pondered words of Scripture. We have not put our curiosity on hold and we have not stopped asking intelligent questions. Of course, for we also serve God with our mind. I hope that through our meditations you have developed a deeper sense of what it means to serve God in the academy and to read the Bible for yourself as an academic.

Much of what I shared on these pages are things I have been taught by others either by listening to people wiser than me or by reading the odd article or book. I could have provided footnotes to books and articles that elaborate on the main ideas discussed. I have resisted doing this because I don't want to give you as a reader a shopping list of things to acquire or give the impression that only by immersing yourself in a pool of Christian literature can you understand Scripture. As a colleague put it, as soon as an academic sees footnotes, they switch to work mode. Instead, I want you to read the Bible slowly and reflectively, by yourself and with others, in the expectation that you will be taught and gain fresh insight (but then read some good books too!). There is benefit to be had from being exposed directly to the words of Scripture that no Christian writing can emulate (including the one you hold in your hand right now). But there are still many books out there that have helped me to see more in Scripture. Two people connected to Tyndale House, Cambridge, the research institute where I work, have written valuable works that express particularly well the same attitude to the Bible as is found in this book. I recommend Peter J. Williams's *Can We Trust the Gospels?* and *The Surprising Genius of Jesus*, which show how paying attention to details opens up layer after layer of intricate connections in Scripture.[1] Christopher Ash's four-volume commentary on Psalms (Crossway, 2024) does heavy lifting and also demonstrates how a radical Christ-centred approach to God's word can teach and transform us by changing the way we think and read.[2]

I owe a debt of gratitude to many people who have been instrumental in bringing this project to a conclusion, not all of whom are mentioned here. I have already mentioned my mentor Bruce Winter, of course. This book is for him. Greg Pritchard has been bugging me for years to write it. O. Palmer Robertson has been a most meaningful encouragement. Brad Green, Peter Williams, Simon Sykes, Christopher Ash, Howard Spencer, Caleb Howard, Ruth Norris and Marion Jongkind have all contributed to it in one way or another, not always consciously. There is no better place to share the goodness of God's word than in the Tyndale House community at Cambridge. Tom Creedy of Inter-Varsity Press has been a great practical help.

How does one measure the success of this book? Not by sales or the number of thank you letters and not by its rank in a citation index. Its success will depend on how it directly or indirectly affects the life of the mind of you as a Christian academic. Only to God be the glory.

Tyndale House, Cambridge

1 Peter J. Williams, *Can We Trust the Gospels?* (Wheaton, IL: Crossway, 2018); Peter J. Williams, *The Surprising Genius of Jesus: What the Gospels Reveal about the Greatest Teacher* (Wheaton, IL: Crossway, 2023).

2 Christopher Ash, *The Psalms: A Christ-Centered Commentary*, 4 vols. (Wheaton, IL: Crossway, 2024).